The Missing Mountain

PHOENIX POETS

MICHAEL COLLIER

The Missing Mountain

New and Selected Poems

THE UNIVERSITY OF CHICAGO PRESS
Chicago and London

The University of Chicago Press, Chicago 60637
The University of Chicago Press, Ltd., London

Published 2021
Printed in the United States of America

30 29 28 27 26 25 24 23 22 21   1 2 3 4 5

ISBN-13: 978-0-226-79525-6 (paper)
ISBN-13: 978-0-226-79539-3 (e-book)
DOI: https://doi.org/10.7208/chicago/9780226795393.001.0001

Library of Congress Cataloging-in-Publication Data

Names: Collier, Michael, 1953- author.
Title: The missing mountain : new and selected poems / Michael Collier.
Other titles: Phoenix poets.
Description: Chicago ; London : The University of Chicago Press, 2021. | Series: Phoenix poets | Includes bibliographical references.
Identifiers: LCCN 2020051201 | ISBN 9780226795256 (paperback) | ISBN 9780226795393 (ebook)
Subjects: LCGFT: Poetry.
Classification: LCC PS3553.O474645 M57 2021 | DDC 811/.54—dc23
LC record available at https://lccn.loc.gov/2020051201

♾ This paper meets the requirements of ANSI/NISO Z39.48-1992 (Permanence of Paper).

for KATHERINE

CONTENTS

FROM *DARK WILD REALM* (2006)

FROM *THE LEDGE* (2000)

FROM *THE NEIGHBOR* (1995)

FROM *THE FOLDED HEART* (1989)

FROM *THE CLASP* (1986)

NEW POEMS (2021)

ACKNOWLEDGMENTS

Many thanks to the editors of the following publications in which these poems first appeared:

American Poetry Review: "To the Muse of Dying" and "Winter"
Atlantic: "Goat on a Pile of Scrap Lumber," "Penn Relays," and "Tree beyond Your Window"
Chicago Quarterly Review: "Cyclist Braking for Two Foxes Crossing a Country Road in Early Morning"
Birmingham Poetry Review: "Bluebirds"
B O D Y: "Morning Crows in a Fresh Mown Field before Rain"
Georgia Review: "A Man of Rueful Countenance," "Colloquy with a Polish Aunt," "Our Felix Randal," and "Today I Can Write"
The Hopkins Review: "A True Story about a Cat and a Possum" and "For a Sixtieth Birthday"
Ploughshares: "In Life"
Poetry Northwest: "His Highness's Dog at Kew"

"Portrait of Two Young Couples" and "The Salvation of America" first appeared in *The Eloquent Poem: 128 Contemporary Poems and Their Making*, edited by Elise Paschen (New York: Persea Books, 2019).

"Aquarium," "White Strawberries," "In Khabarovsk," "Bruges," "Two Girls in a Chair," and "The Clasp" from *The Clasp*, copyright 1986 by Michael Collier. Published by Wesleyan University Press and reprinted with permission.

"North Corridor," "Spider Tumor," "Burial," "The Problem," "The Heavy Light of Shifting Stars," "Feedback," and "The Cave" from *The Folded Heart*, copyright 1989 by Michael Collier. Published by Wesleyan University Press and reprinted with permission.

"Argos," "My Crucifixion," "The Word," "The Farrier," "Ghazal," "All Souls," "Brave Sparrow," "Pay-Per-View," "Cerberus," and "Pax Geologica" from *The Ledge*, copyright 2000 by Michael Collier. Reprinted by permission of Houghton Mifflin Harcourt Publishing Company. All rights reserved.

"Birds Appearing in a Dream," "Confessional," "Summer Anniversary," "Bird Crashing into Window," "The Watch," "The Missing Mountain," "Singing, 5 A.M.," "Mine Own John Clare," "Elegy for a Long-Dead Friend" "A Line from Robert Desnos Used to Commemorate George 'Sonny' Took-the-Shield, Fort Belknap, Montana," and "Bardo" from *Dark Wild Realm*, copyright 2006 by Michael Collier. Reprinted by permission of Houghton Mifflin Harcourt Publishing Company. All rights reserved.

"An Individual History," "My Mother of Invention," "Grandmother with Mink Stole, Sky Harbor Airport, Phoenix, Arizona, 1959," "Cyclops," "At the End of a Ninetieth Summer," "Brendan's Hair," "Piety," "Doctor Friendly," "History," "Rabid Head," "The Bees of Deir Kifa," "Embrace," "Laelaps," and "Six Lines for Louise Bogan" from *An Individual History*, copyright 2012 by Michael Collier. Used by permission of W. W. Norton and Company, Inc.

I'm grateful for the editors I've worked with over the years and thank them for their encouragement: Jeannette Hopkins at Wesleyan University Press; Randy Petilos at the University of Chicago Press; Janet Silver at Houghton Mifflin Harcourt; and Jill Bialosky at W. W. Norton and Company. I thank stalwarts in life and art Charles Baxter, David Biespiel, Maud Casey, Jennifer Grotz, Edward Hirsch, Garrett Hongo, Sally Keith, Jim Longenbach, Tom Mallon, John Murphy, Patrick Phillips, Buzz Poverman, Alan Shapiro, Tom Sleigh, Elizabeth Spires, Ellen Bryant Voigt, and Josh Weiner. And I thank my family for their love: David, Emma Claire, Kay, Robert, and William.

from My Bishop and Other Poems (2018)

MEADOW

Moments that were tender—if I can use that word—now rendered in memory's worn face, have names attached and, less vivid, places that are more frequented than present places. Four decades is not so long ago, when facing an open window, hands braced against the sill (moonlight on *her* back) and, outside, grass in furrows, or so it seems to me who's never left for long that window or looked much beyond the meadow and yet have continually wondered what she was looking at, having never, as far as I can see, looked back.

MY BISHOP

The summer of high school graduation I felt God was calling me to the priesthood.

What I mean by "calling" is not that he spoke to me in a language I understood but that he had given me access to immense and ecstatic experiences of love and joy, not real experiences but ones I perceived as if a limitless future was inside me, as if, and this is why it seemed like a "calling," I was

being invited to see the world that lay behind and beyond the one we are born into.

I began to kneel in my bedroom and pray, not prayers I had been taught but rather ones that inhabited me and for which I was their instrument.

Sometimes as I prayed the sun would come down out of the sky and compress into a flower.

Sometimes people I did not know materialized in the room and prayed with me, and how glad and comforted I was by that intimacy.

Sometimes the prayers were like violent caresses and I would masturbate.

I was eighteen and wanting to live a life filled with meaning, I wrote one of my Jesuit High School teachers about entering the Order.

What he told me was that I should listen not to the voice coming from inside me or the voice from the world beyond but I should listen to the voice coming from the physical world.

He said, God is immanent, everywhere, open, and available.

—

Bishop, my first thought when I saw you enter the funeral home chapel for
my father's Rosary was that you peroxide your hair and then as you came
nearer how little changed by time your face seemed, except a single bangle
of a double chin, but no age lines, no grotesque enlargement of ears and

nose, just a smooth, worriless, mild, unreadable, Irish countenance and that
gingery hair, incongruous in a man so plain.

A fondness for you stirred in me not as a kind of pity for what you'd become
but for what I realized you'd always been: a short, insecure man with a
compassionate heart, proficient at following directions but lacking the
common touch—and whose timidity was now a form of cowardice?

—

What a beautiful detail, what a fine recollection to nudge me with in front of my father's coffin—that you watched the *Smothers Brothers* for the first time when my parents invited you for a Sunday dinner.

Was remembering that show a way of getting a conversation going after forty years, a quick nod to something we'd shared and then on to the real subject?

And what would that have been, the real subject?

What I remember is that you let my father celebrate alone the sacrament of cocktail hour, the way he did most nights: on the counter a bar towel folded just so on which to rest a long, small stirring spoon, its handle topped with a ceramic cherry.

Drink in hand, paper coaster at the ready, he'd watch the news, while from the hallway a gilt-framed, papal marriage blessing with its holy-card cameo of Pius XII admonished him.

In our house nothing was done without the Pope looking on, like the time semi–*in flagrante* on the living room floor with a girl I looked up and there he was, *Papa,* in his white *zucchetto.*

—

For your episcopal motto you chose "To Build Up the Body of Christ," apt for the once young, friendly priest and team chaplain, who lifted weights at the Universal Gym next to the K-Mart on West Indian School Road, who never stopped reminding us to play fair, who even in his cassock could

dribble, fake, and set a shot, or spiral a football, and whose wry, almost cheerful expression met us in the sacristy when, as Knights of the Altar, we'd flip on the white row of switches that lighted up the church, flooding the dark processionary of the nave, reflecting off the cold floor of polished

stone like the bottom of a stream, a fine relief of gray blue, gravel and pebbles—the light all at once expelling the shadows, the vacant spaces that left me calm, certain of purpose, as I filled cruets with wine and water, slipping the folded, starched purificator between the crystal vessels

on their glass tray, while you vested, whispering in Latin: "Gird me, O Lord, with the cincture of purity, and quench in my heart the fire of concupiscence, that the virtue of continence and chastity may abide in me."

So many snippets of prayers, spells of liturgy, Latin and English, parables and miracles—the coal we lit to burn the incense; the clang of the chain against the thurible; bowing, genuflecting, crossing ourselves—all of it abides in me still, serene now, vivid in the radiance of my disbelief.

—

And while the fire in your heart had been quenched, it was not so for the other assistant pastor, Robert B. Gluch, who had charge of the Knights.

Twenty-eight of us in cassocks and surplices, hands steepled as we stood tiered on the altar steps, Gluch not quite in the center at the back, taller by a head, and wearing an ornate cape with a clasp.

Four of us with closed eyes, six of us smirking, including myself.

McDonogh and Braun eyeless behind the reflected glare on their spectacles.

Gluch beatific, head tilted, a male Mary.

—

When my mother saw my father laid out in his rented casket, she asked, in her deaf-person's, loud *sotto voce,* "Who did that to Bob?" And then, "He looks awful!"

And yet, Bishop, for you, she was all false kindness.

"How did you find us?" she wanted to know, as if your presence was both mystery and miracle, and then through the cloud of her dementia, she asked it again, then again and again.

And so, with my mother perseverating and with the waxworks version of my father behind us, and gathered all around—my wife and children, my sisters, brothers-in-law, nephews and nieces, my parents' nona- and octogenarian friends, my dearest childhood friends gathered all around . . .

you turned from her, as if she wasn't speaking, to ask if I was "right with the church," and then because "it would please your father," you offered to hear my confession, whenever I was ready.

—

Pacing back and forth between the white-lined spaces of the parish parking lot, holding his breviary in front of him like a dowser, Gluch would recite his daily offices, and like a shark, when his head turned his body followed.

Once, as I was cutting through the playground to avoid him, he caught my eye and waved me over.

In what must have seemed play to others, he put his arms around me and quickly—my hands becoming feet, my feet in their shoes beneath his chin—turned me upside down.

"I hear you're spreading rumors, Collier."

"You better not."

"You better goddamn not."

And then he swung me like a pendulum.

—

In his letter to Can Grande, Dante describes the meaning of the *Divine Comedy* as not only the state of souls after death but also God's justice as it's manifested in those souls.

Paolo and Francesca forever buffeted by the storm of their lust are caught up in a whirlwind that brings them together, even as it sends them apart.

Can Grande was Dante's benefactor. His name means "Big Dog."

Like you he was an eminence but unlike you he was loved *and* feared.

—

Of course, I wasn't "right" with the church.

But then as if I needed to convince you I was a good man who had lived an ethical life, I introduced you to my wife and sons.

Did that give you a larger opening into my soul?

Is that why you offered to hear my confession, as if you knew it was only a matter of time before I'd come to recognize the need for a particular kind of repentance?

—

All those priests you moved unbeknownst from parish to parish, I see them in Hell, wearing their genitals around their necks instead of the white collars of their office, and the darkness, at least in this circle, is the dark of a black light in which certain textures irradiate a violet shimmer.

In this atmosphere you see what they wear before you see them. By "you" I mean you, Bishop, for having shielded them in life, I've put you in their eternal fraternity.

And where might you put me?

In the narrow, deep crack between belief and disbelief, with those who keep their heads above its chasm by spreading out their arms so their bodies dangle in the emptiness between?

—

I couldn't agree more, Bishop, no one wants to hear a description of human genitals.

The first adult penis I saw was my father's, flaccid, hanging from him as he shaved, right at the level of my face, like three pieces of unfamiliar fruit, the one in the center, peeled, free of its hairy rind, the end of which smooth and purplish was similar to mine but so much bigger it imposed

on me an image of what my body might become, gargantuan, foreign, and accompanied by terrifying demands.

—

What I feared about Gluch was that he knew something about me I didn't know and that's why when he called my mother with an invitation for me to go overnight with him to the Grand Canyon, although she'd already consented, I refused.

But more powerful than the fear of what he might have known about me was the fear that if I went with him, I'd be forever on the other side of my life, even if he didn't fondle me or suck my dick, and I was afraid, too, shame would come between the admiration I had for you, Bishop, and

the loyalty that went with it.

I refused, I refused, I refused.

How easily he had turned my mother into my betrayer.

For decades this event was like a dark black space between her and me.

Several years ago, as I was watching the evening news with her, your face rose up from the depths of the screen, like an image in a Magic 8 Ball.

In her habit of talking to the TV, she asked, "What do they do to those boys?"

"Oral sex, Mom," I said, "oral sex."

—

My father needed a presentable shirt for his viewing so I went to Sears the day before and took a long time deciding if I should buy the fifteen-dollar polyester-cotton blend or spend five more for the all-cotton.

—

The girl I was making out with under Pius XII's watchful eye—if she had pleaded with me to stop, to get off her, "now," if she'd pushed me away, would I?

—

Creeping up from behind us in the sacristy, Gluch enfolded me and another server, as we were called, inside his chasuble, and mimicking Count Dracula invited us to come into his castle where he would show us something.

In a fake, cowering voice, the other boy said, "What are you going to show us father?" and then we both slipped out from beneath his arms.

I had been silent, wary, uncertain of what to do, and yet the other server knew in an instant how to make a joke of it and escape.

And yet both of us had been under his wing, so to speak—altar boy to priest, servant to master, sheep to shepherd, penitent to confessor.

Later, when I was carrying the cruets of wine and water out to the sanctuary, the hem of my cassock made a brisk sibilance as it brushed the tops of my shoes, a sound like a voice that said, as I hear it now, "Tenderness is in us all."

—

Last night, I was on a train, sitting at a table in the dining car with my friend Tom.

I was wearing a black cassock, unbuttoned along its length, collarless.

When you appeared, your cassock buttoned, collar hidden, except for the tooth-sized tab at the front, Tom and I were talking.

Around your neck hung a cross, decorated with inlaid turquoise.

How odd, I thought, that you've found me attired like this, in a dream, posing as a cleric.

I explained to Tom that you had been like a father to me—no pun intended—and how your hands on my shoulders once steadied me, as well as another acolyte, before the three of us exited the sacristy, crossed the sanctuary, and processed down the aisle to the vestibule, to meet a mother, father,

and infant in their coffins.

And then with some sadness and apropos of what I don't know I opened a briefcase, took out a newspaper—the *New York Times,* June 17, 2003—and read: "Beleaguered by a sexual misconduct scandal involving clergy, [the bishop of Phoenix] was arrested Monday in connection with a fatal

hit-and-run accident. . . . he was driving the car Saturday and thought he hit a dog or cat or someone threw a rock. . . . the bishop made phone inquiries about replacing his damaged windshield before police confronted him."

Tom wanted to know if you were the pedophile I'd told so many stories about over the years.

"No, this is the good priest," I said. "The one who became Bishop."

Then Tom wanted to know if Gluch had ever molested me.

Before I could respond, I saw that you were crying.

Not because I wanted to but because it's what's done, I put my arm around you.

"If you thought it was a dog or cat, why didn't you stop?" Tom asked.

"I'm not crying for the dog," you said, impatiently.

"I'm crying because Gluch was a good priest."

—

In Gluch's obituary parishioners at Saint Odelia's, his last posting before he died, remembered him with great fondness.

Perhaps that's all we can hope for, to be remembered with fondness.

—

I meant to say that when your face appeared on the television, my mother first remarked, “He’s not a bright man,” and then I told her what was done to those boys.

—

When my father was an altar boy, he had a bishop who gave him (this was the Depression) a dollar or two, sometimes a five, after serving Mass, meant not for him, it was understood, but for his family who'd "lost everything," as the phrase goes.

In my father's version of the story, his bishop performed an act of charity that allowed my father to save face and required nothing from him but trust.

—

In my version of the story, well, Bishop, why don't you tell me what happens in my version of the story?

—

Fondness aside, when you showed up at the funeral home, I realized how much I disliked you, which surprised me, and not even the grief I felt for my father could forgive it.

I thought to myself, Why do you think you can just show up here?

Who do you think you are?

—

In my version of the story, four years pass and my Bishop shows up at my mother's funeral.

He's pushing a walker with squeaky, plastic wheels and fluorescent tennis balls fixed to the back legs.

His face is slack.

A white pharmaceutical rime crusts the corners of his mouth.

His gingery hair is gray.

I follow his slow effort to reach the altar where he presumes he's wanted as a concelebrant but no one has invited him.

At first he won't look at me directly, but when our eyes meet, he administers a fierce, unforgiving stare.

He sees I'll never be ready for confession.

I pity him.

It's what we do.

I pity, dislike, and I'm fond of him.

The truth of this is almost as bearable as the lie.

Later, when I approach the sanctuary to deliver my mother's eulogy, I give him a quick, involuntary wave like a signal of surrender or a sign that recognizes who we were more than forty years ago—frightened boy and less frightened young priest.

From the lectern, before I begin, I thank him publicly for his friendship.

ANECDOTE OF THE PIANO IN THE WOODS

I came upon a piano in the woods.
Its silver casters balanced on three stones.
A harp lay inside the lean-to of its top.

No bench, except the air, which meant
its silence roused the trees.
The leaves were the music's million,

million ears. The limbs, a hundred
thousand raised batons. Pollen was
yellow snow on its lacquered skin.

Like a swinging bridge above a flooded
creek the keys were rippling dominoes,
and the water running beneath,

molded to the shape of stones below,
was an always moving, never changing
melody, a surface score whose swells

and hollows, whose shadows, read
by sight, sounded a chorus of a single note,
that sounded like a piano in the woods.

BRONZE FOOT IN A GLASS CASE

Damascus National Museum, 2007

Basra is a long way off. I walked there once,
along the Euphrates. When I say "I,"
I mean this foot without a leg to lift it.
Step by step I marched.

After Basra, I returned to Palmyra,
"City of Palms," and stood
a century or two in the shadow
of a wall, a foot with hundreds of feet

waiting for men of flesh and blood
to flood the city with violence,
killing everything that walked,
everything with legs and arms and heads.

If you, who are bending close to me,
can look through the glare
of your own reflection, you'll see
the layer of dust at my heel

and the shadows my toes cast
on the baize. This is where
the waiting ends, this is where
the violence recommences—

in the dust and light
that gathers around me—you
who could not see it
until I told you to look.

THE STORM

Our landlord, a federal bureaucrat, would sit in his car
across the street at the end of the month to collect rent.
He had a scarlet birthmark covering his neck
and tinting the lobe of his left ear. That's what
you got for $125 a month on Capitol Hill
in 1981, a landlord afraid to enter his own building
and a three-hundred-square-foot "garden" apartment.

I did odd jobs for him, painting the long, dark
brick passageway that went past our door,
into the concrete yard and unpaved eeriness of the alley,
and twice repaired locks on apartments upstairs
that had been burglarized. One victim, a newly divorced
woman in her midthirties who lived above us, broke her lease
and moved out. She had dark hair in a style more suitable
for someone much older, combed over on top to disguise a thin spot.
In my mother's parlance, she seemed "ill-equipped to deal with life."

When I called the landlord to say she had "vacated the premises,"
a phrase that came out of my mouth involuntarily, he was silent
for several seconds before calling her a "fuck."
I thought she'd done the right thing considering how
shaken she was and that, among other things, as I was installing
a dead bolt, she said it felt as if she'd been raped; actually,
she used the phrase "gang raped," which seemed hyperbole
to me until I told my wife who without pausing said of course
that's what you'd feel if you were a woman.

Night or day it was the kind of neighborhood
where if something happened you couldn't trust someone
to come to your aid, like the evening my wife and I
were fixing dinner and heard over the radio's drone,
or perhaps through it, what sounded like shouts and screams
or cries; all three, I guess. Beyond the window we could see
a woman flailing, on her side in the street. By the time I reached her
she was up and pointing down the block to a figure running away.
Instinct of a kind I'd never felt sent me after the man
but only the distance of a house or two until another more familiar instinct
sent me back to the woman who was now rubbing the side of her face,
and from instinct, too, I put my arm around her and then,
I don't know how else to say it, she "buried" her face in my shoulder.
"I'm sorry," she said. "I'm so sorry."

—

When one of my sons turned twenty-five, I calculated how old
I would be when he turned fifty, if I were still alive, and then
it occurred to me that after I die his age will begin
to catch up to mine, until at some point in the future,
if he lives long enough, we will for one year
be the same age, the only time in our lives, so to speak,
when I am not keeping ahead of him moving toward death
and he has not yet surpassed me, and in order for me to experience
what he will experience that day, I will have to live until
I'm a month shy of ninety-six, which is how long my father lived.

—

The afternoon the Air Florida jet crashed in the Potomac
I was working in the basement apartment on Tenth Street.
The blizzard had been accompanied by lightning and thunder,
big booms and flashes, as if there were a storm within a storm.

By noon the schoolyard across the street had close to a foot.
One of the many times I got up from my work to look out
the small window, I saw a group of boys tramping slowly
in a jagged file across the playground, each carrying a large

household item: a TV with its cord dragging, a turntable atop
an amplifier, speakers, an IBM typewriter. The last boy dragged
a red plastic sled with a bulky, olive-green duffel bag as freight.
"Burglars in the Snow," I thought, like a Breugel painting.

We lived close enough to National to hear planes land
and take off, intermittent muffled rumblings I'd learned
to ignore, although at first I tracked them tensely
like a passenger strapped in his seat silently urging the plane up.

Back then, I was afraid of so many things. I dealt with fear
by acting brave and impervious, cultivating as well
an ironic bonhomie that covered up the effort.
Everything was an effort, so I made effortlessness my goal.

At night, what I'd avoided during the day appeared
in the form of my child self: a pale, chubby, asthmatic boy
brought too easily to tears, who could not say no for cowardice
the time at the state fair he rode "The Hammer" with an older boy he admired.

Rising in the gondola above the midway with its tantalizing lights,
he felt alive in a peculiar but appealing way as it rocked gently.
For a moment courage was like gaining altitude incrementally
and yet, from having waited his turn in line, he knew what was coming.

If you want to know what fear looks like, look at the boy
when he finishes the ride. He's smiling because he thinks
everyone is watching him, and that's why, too, when his friend suggests
they ride again he keeps smiling and can't believe what he's agreed to do.

—

Along with the hospice nurse, who kept increasing his morphine,
reassuring me she had the orders for upping the dose,
which meant she was hastening his departure, I was with my father when he died.
And yet the nurse, whose name I can't remember, although
I promised myself never to forget, had been trying hard to keep him alive.
She brought out a nebulizer to help him breathe.
"Robert, cough. Cough, Robert," she urged.
He hadn't responded to either of us for several hours, yet we could
hear him struggling to comply or maybe he was trying to speak.
No matter, a few hours later the nurse told me quietly he was near the end
and if family wanted to see him before he passed I should let them know.
What took them so long getting there I didn't ask.
The nurse stayed with us, meaning my father and me, as I kept waiting
for my sisters and brothers-in-law to come through the door or kept hoping
they wouldn't so I would have the moment to myself, not to myself
but for myself, with my father, whose ragged breathing, occasional gasps,
and, yes, coughing, had become thin and shallow, although his fingers roved
over the sheet and even jumped now and then. His head at an angle
on the pillow made it seem as if he was concentrating
extremely hard on the ceiling as if, I thought, he was listening
to someone talking to him from up there and all the effort
he had been expending hour after hour to catch his breath, to let
go of the great sighing his lungs and mouth produced, the heaves
and groans, the agitated restlessness of his body, the unappeasable
shiftings of his discomfort, had left him washed-up, alone
and isolated as the tide, which had been ebbing all night and into
the morning was so far out and had taken with it so much
shore that my father was left on a pedestal of sand, around
which a shallow moat dissipated the further the tide withdrew,
and just as I in my exhaustion believed he was the island
of Mont-Saint-Michel—his head the cathedral nestled in the tightly
clustered village, his nose the spire rising from the bell tower—

just then his utterly blue eyes opened. Shocked by their own awakening they looked at whatever it was they saw, which is why when his eyes closed and he died, his mouth remained open. The last thing the nurse did was to brush, no, to flick his hair up off his forehead.

—

The plane's tail hit the Fourteenth Street bridge, sheared open automobiles
stalled in the storm-clogged traffic, and then went nose first
into the frozen river. Twenty years later, the sister
of one of the crash victims said, "There's a tenacity

the dead have on the living that no living person has on you."
When the rescue helicopter got low enough over the Potomac
the pilot could see through the whiteout a few people standing
on one of the jet's wings. To say the river was frozen

isn't really accurate. It was chockablock with ice floes.
The plane had opened up a lead in the ice between it
and the shore that was covered quickly with jet fuel.

—

For part of the War my father was stationed in DC as a flight controller
at National. Late one night, he guided Charles Lindberg to a landing
and then went on the field to meet him. Since Lindberg
was there only to refuel, they walked among the planes, talking.

For many years, my father carried in his billfold a dollar
Lindberg had signed and given to him. He called it a "short snorter."
This meant if he ever met Lindberg again and couldn't produce the bill,
he'd have to buy him a drink.

When he was first assigned to National, my father lived alone
in an apartment that would eventually house my mother and oldest sister
who were then with family in Indianapolis. One night awakened
by a tapping at the window, he hauled up the blinds to find

a man's legs and feet dangling from above. On the few occasions
I heard him tell this story, he provided little more than
what I've written here. I never thought to ask him, as I'd like to now,
what effect discovering that man had on his life.

I'd like to know, too, if he ever thought about killing himself.
A day rarely passes without my college roommate,
Jimmy O'Loughlin, who asphyxiated himself in his father's car,
coming into my thoughts or appearing in his bell-bottoms

and flowery shirts, hair teased and ratted like Rod Stewart's
and his side of the room littered with crushed packs of KOOLs
and discarded cups of Laura Scudder vanilla pudding,
which he used to snuff out the butts. What might it mean

that during the semester O'Loughlin began to contemplate his demise,
I was writing an art history paper on Dadaist suicide?
Dada was like throwing a full garbage can into someone's backyard
or swimming pool, something I did with friends in high school.

We called it "alley aping." And Dada suicide was an act of such
nonchalance and indifference that I mistook it for courage.
When Giacometti was asked, "Have you ever thought of suicide?"
he replied, "I think of it every day, but not because I find life intolerable,

not at all, rather because I think death must be a fascinating
experience." That's not how I think of suicide. I think of it
as one among many solutions to the problem of living,
different than the others, all of which involve staying alive.

Freud said it is impossible to imagine our own deaths,
he who imagined his down to its exact dosage in morphine.
When O'Loughlin climbed inside his father's car
and started it up in the garage, he had moved home to finish

two incompletes so he could graduate with our class,
that was his particular problem of living.

—

Twenty years ago, when I first wrote about the crash,
I began, “So, you were in a cave of your own making.”
Meaning the three hundred square feet of apartment where,
after my wife left for work, I rolled up the foam mat

we slept on, brought a chair in from the other room,
and worked at a narrow, plywood desk, a desk lamp
the only light, warm and intimate, but intense
and clarifying for the way it invited concentration.

And then I wrote: “You got up from the desk
And walked to the window covered by security bars.”
That’s when I saw the boys crossing the playground.
My first thought was “Burglars in the Snow” because

I’d been memorizing John Berryman’s “Winter Landscape,”
which is based on Breugel’s *The Hunters in the Snow.*
As I looked through the bars at the freezing world,
what should have been a quiet scene shook with thunder

and was lit up with clouds that pulsed with lightning.
I recited the poem silently, slowly, and imperfectly,
as if I were lip-synching sounds I heard in my head.
Sometimes I repeated the previous line to get to the next.

Here’s the middle of the poem:

> Are not aware that in the sandy time
> To come, the evil waste of history
> Outstretched, they will be seen upon the brow
> Of that same hill: when all their company
> Will have been irrecoverably lost,
>
> These men, this particular three in brown
> Witnessed by birds will keep the scene . . .

The woman who had been mugged had written her
phone number and name on a scrap of paper I had torn
from a yellow legal pad I used for writing, and for several months
I kept it folded in my wallet. If I called her I'd be setting

in motion events beyond my control, which is what
I must have wanted, but not enough. Occasionally, I'd take it out.
It reminded me of how when I put my arm around her
I also brushed away her hair from her face with my fingers

and curled it behind her ear to stay in place.

—

The mnemonic that recalls the address of the Capitol Hill apartment
behind the Marine barracks on Eighth Street, SE, that billeted
the drum and bugle corps and honor guards for State functions
the year my wife and I lived in DC (747 Tenth Street) is *Jumbo Jet*.
Four stories of watery-green brick, tallest on a block that marked
the edge of a neighborhood's stalled gentrification. Fall into early spring
on Friday nights we could hear the sounds of the bands fade in and out
as if on a tide. Cannons going off ricocheted inside the parade ground
announced the ceremony's end. Our windows hummed, and once
a small jade horse stationed on a shelf fell over and broke a hoof.
The bands were called the Commandant's Own and the President's Own.

—

O'Loughlin was in Yale Psychiatric Institute recovering from
an earlier suicide attempt when on Tuesday, October 13, 1970,
the day Bobby Seale was appearing in New Haven for a pretrial
hearing as the accused for the murder of a fellow Black Panther,
O'Loughlin phoned in a bomb threat but didn't specify
why or where so the police evacuated three courthouses.

At our tenth college reunion I said to Betty, his
former girlfriend, that if Jimmy had only known
how much he was loved . . . "Are you kidding," she said.
"Give me a fucking break. He knew he was loved."

—

One night, a few days after the crash, I was driving back
from a party, late, alone, on the George Washington Parkway,
which because of high-banked snow was like a shallow,
roofless tunnel. Headlights reflected off the opposite side

of the road as I came into a turn, a blue-white, arctic
shimmer and as such the dark, clear night above pressed down,
or so it seemed, as if it had physical weight, but when the road
made a wide, broad turn, and with the shoulders plowed

on either side flush to the pavement, the river came into view
and across it the dome of the Jefferson. Up ahead, brighter
than day, towers of high-intensity floodlights lit up
the near end of the bridge. Suspended in the illumination,

rising by cable up a crane and dripping with water, was the tail
of the plane, growing larger but stranger as I drew closer.
Stranger because it was exactly what it appeared to be, or I should say
what I expected it to be, but at the same time it was larger,

monumental, a warrior's shield inscribed with a runelike logo,
a Celtic or Arabic intertwining riddle, an empire's seal,
so much shaped metal, trapezoidal, hanging, twisting
as it came to a stop. But it wasn't until I was heading

into the District on the undamaged span that it became fully
what it was, torn off its body, a wounded appendage, an explosion
of peeled-back skin, bone and tendon and arteries severed, distended,
and no mnemonic or involuntary phrase to repair or rename what it was,

not a link in the chain of modern disasters, not a harbinger of wrecks
and salvages—the unceasing drone of cranes and claws loading barges
with misshapen beams and miles of wire and glass that hadn't melted—
but a scrap of paper with a name, a power cord dragging in snow,

O'Loughlin hanging up the phone, my father's short snorter,
a bit boring through the door, the airplane picking up speed,
thunder inside of snow, "God, look at that thing,"
one of the pilots said, "that don't look right."

BOOM BOOM

I leave my backyard and enter the alley in search of my poetry. I get lost a few houses down near the Eldridges' because all the fences and trash cans are identical. I am alone filling a shirt pocket with the bees David Hills eviscerates by pulling out their stingers and which he has lined up on a flap torn from a cardboard box that's pinned to the ground with four small stones. In a toolbox I have a small hammer and screwdrivers for taking things apart. Above me is the sky that is always blue. (This means at night the stars are what I see but can't count.) The alley is dirt. My shoes scuff its uneven surface. Suddenly a door opens, a dog barks, it is Boom Boom, a Chihuahua, not even a dog in my mind. It rushes its side of the fence and is so much louder and fiercer than it needs to be. After a while it stops. Now it sounds like a tambourine because of a collar with tiny bells. Passionflowers grow in a thick vine over Boom Boom's fence. I have been told the leaves of these flowers are the lances that pierced Jesus's chest and broke his legs. Boom Boom is whimpering, lying down near a place in the fence through which I squeeze my hand to touch his nose. "Boom Boom," I say, very quietly, "I love you. You are the only one who understands me." Afterwards, I feel very small and very large, restrained and freed, and certain there is a purpose to life beyond the one I've been given.

A WILD TOM TURKEY

When he's in the yard he's hard to find,
not like when he stands in the stubble
across the road brewing his voice

with deeper and deeper percolations
of what sounds like "I'll fuck anything
in feathers," stopping now and then

to display his fan and perform a wobbly
polka, chest heavy as he breasts forward
but never closes on the hens who stay

in wary steps ahead, conversing only
with themselves, their spindly heads foraging,
measuring the distance that frustrates

his occasional flustering leaps so that
when they reach the street, their scurry
provokes him to fly, as if he's both

bull and matador, charging and turning
in the air but landing in a bounding,
rolling heap, which sends the rafter of them

deep into the grass, where after much silence,
what happens sounds like murder.

LEN BIAS, A BOUQUET OF FLOWERS, AND MS. BROOKS

He arrives in the middle of her reading. She
has to stop and, taking the flowers he's brought, kisses
the beautiful young man whose yellow socks are her
dowdy sweater's antithesis. What's said between them is killed
by applause, but not his smile, which is the smile of a boy
standing in the silence he's created, and
not her magnified stare, which says she
understands why he's arrived late, is
already leaving, and that he is sorry.

LAST MORNING WITH STEVE ORLEN

"Last Night I wrote a Russian novel or maybe it was English.
Either way, it was long and boring. My wife's laughter
might tell you which it was, and when she stops,
when she's not laughing, let's talk about the plot
and its many colors. The blue that hovered in the door
where the lovers held each other but didn't kiss.
The red that by mistake rose in the sky with the moon,
and the moon-colored sun that wouldn't leave the sky.
All night I kept writing it down, each word arranged
in my mouth, but now, as you can see, I'm flirting
with my wife. I'm making her laugh. She's twenty.
I'm twenty-five, just as we were when we met, just
as we have always been, except for last night's novel,
Russian or English, with its shimmering curtain of color,
an unfading show of northern lights, what you, you asshole,
might call *aurora borealis.*
So sit down on the bed with my wife and me.
Faithful amanuensis, you can write down my last words,
not that they're great but maybe they are.
You wouldn't know. You're an *aurora borealis.*
But my wife is laughing and you're laughing too.
Just as we were at the beginning, just as we are at the end."

from An Individual History (2012)

AN INDIVIDUAL HISTORY

This was before the time of lithium and Zoloft

before mood stabilizers and anxiolytics

and almost all the psychotropic drugs, but not before Thorazine,

which the suicide O'Loughlin called "handcuffs for the mind."

It was before, during, and after the time of atomic fallout,

Auschwitz, the Nakba, DDT, and you could take water cures,

find solace in quarantines, participate in shunnings,

or stand at Lourdes among the canes and crutches.

It was when the March of Time kept taking off its boots.

Fridays when families prayed the Living Rosary

to neutralize communists with prayer.

When electroshock was electrocution

and hammers recognized the purpose of a nail.

And so, if you were as crazy as my maternal grandmother was then

you might make the pilgrimage she did through the wards

of state and private institutions,

and make of your own body a nail for pounding, its head

sunk past quagmires, coups d'etat, and disappearances

and in this way find a place in history

among the detained and unparoled, an individual like her,

though hidden by an epoch of lean notation—"Marked

Parkinsonian tremor," "Chronic paranoid type"—

a time when the animal slowed by its fate

was excited to catch a glimpse of its tail

or feel through her skin the dulled-over joy

when for a moment her hands were still.

MY MOTHER OF INVENTION

The needle goes up and down on my mother's Singer,
squat black with its gold scroll and script,
shaped like a smokestack turned on its side.

Have you ever seen a dipper bobbing in a stream?
It's like the Singer but so much slower. Its beak
makes thread of water and sews patterns of spreading ripples.

Such a fierce engine at the center of creation
and beautifully sculpted, a porcelain boot
or a falconer's gauntlet. The dipper likes the action

of a cataract, the rapid tumble of rapids,
and if it wants walks easily along the stream's pebbly bottom.
Hour after hour, my mother's fingers fed the fabric

through the pressing foot, kept the seams flat,
while thread spooled out and the bobbin coaxed up
from its metal gear held the stitch.

The American Dipper? What joy in finding such a bird.
Its short trills punctuated by sharp, clear *zeets.*
Its eyelid white against total gray, when it blinks.

If it didn't exist, you'd have to make it up.
You'd have to give it its own day of creation,
a day of translucent patterns, pinking shears, and pins.

You'd have to say, come see how the sewing machine
in its sleek skin dips and bobs and swims,
and how my mother, white eyelid lined blue,

sings her same stitched tune—never remembered
so never heard—and how like a solitary
calls out, not in air but under water.

GRANDMOTHER WITH MINK STOLE, SKY HARBOR AIRPORT, PHOENIX, ARIZONA, 1959

It rode on her shoulders
flayed in its purposes of warmth and glamour.

Its head like a small dog's and its eyes
more sympathetic than my mother's eyes' kindness

which was vast. Four paws for good luck
but also tiny sandbags of mortification and ballast,

and in the black claws a hint of brooch or clasp.
Secured like that the head could loll and the teeth

in the snout's fixed grin was the clenched "Oh, shit!"
of road kill askew in the gutter. This she wore

no matter the weather and always, always,
when she stepped from the plane and paused,

at the top of the rolling stairs, she fit her hand
to her brow against the glare of concrete and desert,

not a white glove's soft salute but a visor
that brought us into focus. Mother and Father waving first,

then oldest to youngest, dressed in our Easter best,
we were prodded to greet her, she who gripped the hot,

gleaming rail, set her teeth in the mink's stiff grin
and walked through the waterless, smokeless mirage between us.

She who wore the pelt, the helmet of blue hair
and came to us mint and camphor-scented, more strange

than her unvisited world of trees and seasons,
offering us two mouths, two sets of lips, two expressions:

the large, averted one we were meant to kiss and the other
small, pleading, that if we had the choice, we might choose.

CYCLOPS

My grandfather's right eye was a frozen slab
of milk-white ice that light never thawed
and when he slept, the lid didn't drown
the curse of its constant stare.

Look at it long and you'd be salt, stone—
fear's hard form. And look we did,
though we blinked against its spell, the worm
or ray or evil thread of its insistence.

I'd watch him read with half his face alive
and the other like a tool, oiled, hanging
from a hook as if you could take it in your hands
and make it work, but you couldn't.

The eye that saw the words counted money,
lit his pipe and bet on horses at the track.
It measured out his evening whiskey and led him
to the thresholds of our rooms to say good night.

O, calm, wheel-eyed giant, you might have tamed us
had we let you hold our hands the way
you wanted or stood beside you closer
when we looked into the sun and forced a smile.

But your hands were colder, more distant than
your gaze, and standing in our doorway your head
was like a moon, vast and disappearing,
occupied by all its phases, and so we tried

to pass unseen, unknown even as we sharpened
and heated the stake of our revulsion
and plotted when to thrust the smoldering tip
not into the eye that roved and guided

but into the one that monitored the smoky,
ice-stung realm inside your skull. Now that you're gone,
lift your curse, look at us more clearly
with whichever eye condones forgiveness.

AT THE END OF A NINETIETH SUMMER

They drink their cocktails in the calm manner
of their middle years, while the dim lights
around the swimming pool make shadows
of that world they've almost fully entered.

Like Yeats's wild swans their uneven number
suggests at least one of them is no longer mated.
Added up, their several ages are short of a millennium.
This means the melting ice cubes are silent music beneath

their slow talk, and slow talk is how gods murmur
when eternity comes to an end.
The way it feels for these friends who amaze themselves
with what they remember—not the small details—

but how long ago lives happened and how fast.
Occasionally, usually from the wives, there's mention
of the War, as if they'd endured before waiting like this,
except now there's no uncertain homecoming,

no life to be beginning and nothing to complete
that doesn't wear already the aura of completion.
Listen, they are laughing. One eases himself up
to refill his drink. His wife, in a wheelchair, wants one, too.

Another makes a joke about making it a double
and gets up to help. They are gone so long,
or not long enough, that someone asks,
"Where's Bob and Jim?"

Now and then a tentacle of the robot vacuum
submerged in the pool breaches the surface,
squirts a welcome spray of water
then retracts where it continues its random sweeps,

until it breaks into the air again.
Bob and Jim are back, the drinks get passed,
even so Jim's wife asks, "Where did you go?"
Instead of answering, he raises his glass.

BRENDAN'S HAIR

And we spent a long time hovering above the sky,
crying on its great canvas surface, tears collecting
in low spots, sagging the fabric through which
the sun usually poured. That's why we went back inside

and took up the brooms to push off the water and drain
the burden our sadness made. That's why we walked up
the aisle holding hands, straight to his white coffin—
a gift from the queen of cold and ice—and his white suit,

the touch of snow on the bruised forehead—icing
from the vault of death—and the white blanket
folded under his gleaming hands, and that's why we didn't linger,
except to register the scalp, albino pink,

and his hair in its last furrows but wrongly parted,
which my son wanted to know from that instant
of seeing his friend in the elaborate bed, he wanted to know:
"Why did they do that to Brendan's hair?"

PIETY

Once I had a good church voice
and having been a Knight of the Altar,
I have impeccable church manners.
I know that sounds superior,
but it's not something I brag about,
rather it's a small, inner satisfaction
and nothing like the superiority
the church organist from my childhood parish
displayed when it came time for him,
the last congregant to take communion,
to climb down from his bench,
exit the sacristy, and through the side chapel
gain the main aisle, all the while
his hands flattened together,
like two soft trowels, arms extended,
elbows turned out, and his head
with its grayish, Liberace pompadour,
thrown back, eyes heavenward.
Any of us who served Mass
knew the inside of his mouth—
bobbed tonsils, missing molars,
silver fillings, and the yellowish, veined,
smoker's tongue hanging over the edge
of his lower lip, moist with holy
adhesive and reptilian in its reach.

DOCTOR FRIENDLY

He was an example of anti-nominal determinism,
though he was friendly in manner, kindly
explaining that my light-headedness
and the cold nausea moving through me
probably, most likely, was the Novocain

he'd shot twice into a vein or vessel,
instead of numbing the surrounding nerves
and tissue—and that's why my heart was racing, too—
but he could try again, though only once more,
for that was all the dose a male my weight could handle.

Maybe, sitting in the chair, blinded by the watery
examination lamp, and still feeling the heavy weight
of the X-ray bib across my chest and abdomen,
I didn't have the distance I needed to make a good decision.
It was like the time I was thrown out the door

of my van on the second or third roll, and landing
somehow conscious but not unscathed in the road,
my only thought was to sit down, right where I was,
just for a moment, to collect myself, which is precisely
what I was doing when a passerby urged me to get up

and go with him to the shoulder of the road.
And that's what I did and that's what Doctor Friendly
should have done, suggested I lie calmly in the chair,
take a minute to compose myself, and then reschedule.
What idiot, blind, fearful, un-numbed part of me

assented to the third injection, I know well,
for who can refrain from administering
the shock or current, cinching the collar, or denouncing
the illiberal rule laid down for the liberal cause?
Who can concede to better judgment and be grateful

for the stranger who leads you from the road
and stays until the cops arrive,
or wave off the final swab of numbing gel,
that brought me to the brink again
beneath Doctor Friendly's masked, hovering face.

HISTORY

When I met the famous *Felix Dzerzhinsky*,
he was a passenger ship and wore
a stiff, riveted smile as he rolled gracefully
over the eastern Pacific's long cold swells.
His head was square, like a stern, while his pigeon-toed feet
formed a bow, and his eyes, shaped like anchors,
moved up and down on chains.
You don't get made into a ship for being a nice man.
You don't become a statue in Lubyanka Square
without some "organized terror."
How else to build a reputation, lay the keel?

On a ship named for such a person,
there might be a man, in his sixties, bald, with a limp,
dressed in tweeds, accompanied by a younger,
much taller, elegant Japanese woman, a man with a name
that's hard to forget, who knows Ancient Greek and Latin,
speaks French, Italian, Spanish, Japanese—his native German—
not to mention English in which you converse.
What makes him think the ship will never reach port,
that he can say the things he says about Russians and Jews?
Or that he can get through customs without opening
his big leather bag, right next to you, with its spare limb.

—

A chessboard was painted on *Dzerzhinsky*'s back,
sand-weighted pieces as tall as five feet and easy
to move into position, but the passage was rough
through the Strait of Tsugaru: rooks, knights, bishops, queens,
and kings fell down and rolled on their pedestals,
like tops, while pawns upright slid around.

Who knows the fate of the U.S.S.R. *Felix Dzerzhinsky*,
perhaps it's a casino aground on the Aral Sea,
or like his socialist-realism sculpture, toppled by a crane.
How bad could he have been? I only knew him as a ship.
We parted after crossing Tokyo Bay under a bright sun,
although it was night in Yokohama, when we arrived,

wharf lights and cranes glared and hovered, and the tugs
that accompanied us nudged *Dzerzhinsky* in place.
Between hull and pier the lap of water was only
an expected sound, not a way of listening to the incessant
future shuttling between the present and the past, trapped
in a narrow channel too small for the ship I myself might be.

—

What kind of man travels the world with an extra leg?
When we said goodbye he gave me his calling card

Dr. Otto Karl Schmidt
Osterwaldstr. 48
D 8000 München 40
Tel. 089/ 4 522 063

and a folded piece of paper on which he'd written a request.
I've saved the Christmas card he sent in thanks.

On the front is a painting by a Hugo König,
Beim Türmer von St. Peter, a nineteenth-century scene:
two young girls, sisters, I suppose, stand behind
a head-high iron-work rail on a balcony. The older sister
wears gloves and holds onto the rail with one hand,
standing on half tiptoe, looking down—a city snowscape
with steep-pitched roofs and two church bell towers,
above which a flock of almost indistinct crows circles.
The younger sister, blond curls escaping from her winter bonnet,
looks into the sky, away from the city, or perhaps at a spire
that rises behind them. Unlike her sister, she wears
a woolen jacket, and as if dizzy from looking up so long,
her ungloved, left hand grips her sister's jumper.
(The grip is tight because Hönig painted
gathers on the fabric.) The scene must be so famous
most Germans, especially of a given age, would know
exactly what draws the younger girl's attention. Yes,
Saint Peter's tower, and the towers across the way,
patrolled by crows: the venerable Frauenkirche's.

Inside, a printed salutation reads:

> Frohe / Weihnacten / und/ ein gutes / neues Jahr

followed, in a tight neat hand:

> *Wishes you, dear Michael,*
> *Your Transib-Companion, Otto Karl*

and

> *. . . indeed you did me an enormous favor by digging up again KRIVITSKY'S "WHY STALIN SHOT HIS GENERALS" and I have been fascinated to read it over again forty years later! Then I had shown it to Ambassador OTT in Tokyo because I thought it was the truth, the German ambassador did not believe in it. Now I know I was right. W. Krivitsky, alias Samuel GINSBERG, a GPU-General sought asylum first in France. Having escaped there 2 attempts on his life, he retreated to Washington, where he was found shot in a hotel on 10th Febr. 1941, two years after that article.*

—

I would have sent parts 2 and 3 of Krivitsky's article
if his Christmas card had not included a Xerox of an excerpt
from *Hog Island and Other Essays* by James J. Martin, a Holocaust denier.
Even so, the decent thing to do was to carry out his favor.

And yet how hard would it have been for him to track down
Krivitsky? The articles ran in *The Saturday Evening Post.*
And Stalin's ruthlessness, he'd already detailed, along with Hitler's
opening of the Eastern Front "to save Europe from the Bolsheviks,"

never mind wolf packs off the coast of the Americas, nor his escape
from Dachau, where he was confined after the war—
this man whose motto was *Veritas est magna et praevalebit*—
and spent his retirement defending fascists like Leon Degrelle,

and publishing a book, *Pearl Harbor in neuer Sicht.*

—

When I met the famous *Felix Dzerzhinsky*,
he was a ship on the cover of an Intourist brochure
and not the one I sailed on from Siberia to Japan.
The ship I sailed, the U.S.S.R. *Baikal*, was a lake,
and how a lake could be a ship, I don't understand,
and I don't understand Michael Collier, then or now,
who loves the idea that truth is great. He'll never be a ship or a lake.
He'll never have a cable cinched around his neck—never, never,
never!—pulled, head to pedestal, to the ground and cut up for scrap.
When he traveled the world in 1977, what was he thinking?
He wasn't. He was dreaming, like he is now—waking and sleeping,
watching himself throw Romanian lei from the window
of a train approaching the Russian border. He had more of it
than he could account for and was afraid.

—

Before I met the U.S.S.R. *Baikal*, I took a train
from Bucharest to Moscow and from there
to Nahodka, Russia's Pacific port for foreigners.

In "soft class," the car's conductor brought us tea, morning
and afternoon, in glass cups with metal handles, sugar cubes,
and sweet crackers, that's all the comfort he'd been trained to give.

Otherwise he hectored us with gestures and disdained anyone
who boarded after Moscow. One night, he beckoned me
to his compartment. I knew four Russian words: "thank you,"
    "yes," "no," and "closed."

Everything was closed in that vast country, meaning "broken"—
"Za-groo-ta" is what it sounded like, and that night,
after many thimbles of vodka, I learned the word

for what it means to embrace the opposite of what you hate,
even if in essence it's just the same. "Hard-to-show" is what I heard
as he gave thumbs up to Pinochet, Baby Doc, and Franco,

and also, nodding to the corridor, where the man and his
tall companion stood, he repeated a word I didn't understand
until he took my pen and drew a swastika on his skin.

RABID HEAD

so ponderous, it must be the problem he can't solve:
how to carry the bone-cage, the crash helmet for eyes,
and raccoon brain, how to keep the flange-like cheeks
aligned, nose working a proper snuffle

and the dark mask from slipping
or the tail's rings regulated and the black ink scribbling
a legible path from its fine claws, but here
on the side of the road, caught out in the light-storm of midday,

he seems to shake the glare of asphalt off his face
before he steps into the street—the heavy dowser
of his nose pulling his quaking, dithering body
near the mortal blur of traffic, and stopping

not to sniff or reconnoiter but to find the storm drain's iron mask
set into the curb and gutter through which he'll disappear.

THE BEES OF DEIR KIFA

The sun going down is lost in the gorge to the south,
lost in the rows of olive trees, light in the webs of their limbs.

This is the time when the thousands and thousands come home.
It is not the time for the keeper's veil and gloves,

not the time for stoking the smoker with pine needles.
It would be better to do that at midday, under a hot sun,

when the precincts are quieter; it would be better to disturb
few rather than many. At noon, the hives are like villages,

gates opened toward the sun or like small countries
carved from empires to keep the peace, each with its habits—

some ruled better by better queens, some frantic and uncertain,
some with drifting populations, others busy with robbing,

and even the wasps and hornets, the fierce invaders who have settled
among the natives, are involved in the ancient trades.

But now with the sun gone, the blue summer twilight
tinged with thyme and the silver underside of olive leaves

calm in the furrowed groves, darkening the white chunks
of limestone exposed in the tillage, the keeper in his vestments

squeezes the bellows of the smoker, blows a thin blue stream
into an entrance, loosens the top, like a box lid, and delivers more.

For a while, the hive cannot understand what it says to itself.
Now a single Babel presides in the alleys and passageways

and as block by block, the keeper takes his census,
he could go ungloved, unveiled, if it weren't for the unpacified,

the unconfused, returning, mouths gorged with nectar,
legs orange with pollen, landing, amassing, alerting the lulled

to scale their wax trellis or find the glove's worn thumb, the hood's
broken zipper and plant the eviscerating stinger.

EMBRACE

The great flowery dress of my seventh-grade teacher,
cotton or rayon, pillowcase for her vast
mothering bosom, scented with the perfume
of the unmarried, stretched over hips
that made arms of the lap I sat on—
you were the handkerchief of my remorse
just once, you with your bright roses and tulips,
spidery paths of vines and fluted leaves,
all the smothering penance that nearly consoled me,
until above my sobs I heard hers
and in her arms the crushing force
or the grateful fury of our unburdening
made that embrace a thing apart:
O heartsick woman! O bewildered boy!

LAELAPS

When it was clear I would never catch her
and that she would never escape my pursuit,
Zeus intervened and turned each of us to stone.

No longer was ardor our fate. No longer
were days marked by bramble giving way to bog,
by razory reeds that cut our swift passing.

Days when all I saw of her was airborne,
arrowy—a silvery shimmer and flash of scut.
And gone, too, the late-night stillness

when I'd pause, not thinking to lose her,
but hoping, ahead of my silence,
she'd slow down and turning, see,

snout up, tongue lively, lightly panting,
undiscouraged, how at the edge of our distance
I stood, wishing she'd invite my approach.

But these are dog thoughts and I was god's
hound by way of Europa, Minos, and Procris,
so much passing on of love's troubles

I was meant to end. Who wouldn't want to die
into monumental stillness? Who wouldn't want
to be frozen in their last untaken step, translated,

like we were—my pointer's stance, her backward
glance—in the vast sky, where the gods below
had safely placed us?

SIX LINES FOR LOUISE BOGAN

All that has tamed me I have learned to love
    and lost that wildness that was once beloved.

All that was loved I've learned to tame
    and lost the beloved that once was wild.

All that is wild is tamed by love—
    and the beloved (wildness) that once was loved.

from Dark Wild Realm (2006)

BIRDS APPEARING IN A DREAM

One had feathers like a blood-streaked koi,
another a tail of color-coded wires.
One was a blackbird stretching orchid wings,
another a flicker with a wounded head.

All flew like leaves fluttering to escape,
bright, circulating in burning air,
and all returned when the air cleared.
One was a kingfisher trapped in its bower,

deep in the ground, miles from water.
Everything is real and everything isn't.
Some had names and some didn't.
Named and nameless shapes of birds,

at night my hand can touch your feathers
and then I wipe the vernix from your wings,
you who have made bright things from shadows,
you who have crossed the distances to roost in me.

CONFESSIONAL

I was waiting for the frequency of my attention
to be tuned to an inner station—all mind but trivial matter,
wavelengths modulated like topiary swans on a topiary sea,
and not quite knowing where the tide would take me.

In the darkness where I kneeled, I heard whispering,
like dry leaves. It had a smell—beeswax, smoke;
a color—black; and a shape like a thumb.
That's when the door slid open and the light that years ago

spoke to me, spoke again, and through the veil,
an arm, like a hand-headed snake, worked through,
seven-fingered, each tipped with sin. What the snake couldn't see,
I saw, even as it felt what I felt or heard what I said.

Then along my arms boils and welts rose, on my back
scourge marks burned. I counted nails, thorns.
In my mind, inside my own death's head, I could hear: "Please,
forgive me. Do not punish me for what I cannot be."

SUMMER ANNIVERSARY

It was the night before the anniversary
of your death and the dream I had
was not of you but of a neighbor
who the day before had undergone some tests.

He stood in his yard holding a rake
the size of a palm frond.
The grass was brown and the leaves
on all the trees hung as they do in summer,

patiently, not concerned they'll fall.
It was the night before the anniversary
of your death and my neighbor with the rake
had not yet heard the results of his tests

and so he wanted to be ready for the leaves.
He wanted to apologize as well for being
in my dream. He said, "It's not like me
to die." "You're not dying," I told him,

"you're only in my dream." Then he disappeared.
But the rake he'd held stood by itself,
and the grass, now green, grew quickly
up the rake and sculpted a creature

whose wings stretched over me to catch
the falling leaves, for all at once
it was autumn and the sky let loose
its winter fox and then its hound,

though neither moved, and so the space between them
grew, slowly at first, until it was at the speed
of the world, unseen, spinning like time itself,
pushing apart lover and beloved.

BIRD CRASHING INTO WINDOW

In cartoons they do it and then get up,
a carousel of stars, asterisks, and question marks
trapped in a caption bubble above a dizzy,
flattened head that pops back into shape.

But this one collapsed in its skirt of red feathers
and now its head hangs like a closed hinge and its beak,
a yellow dart, is stuck in the gray porch floor
and seems transformed forever—a broken gadget,

a heavy shuttlecock—and yet it's not all dead.
The breast palpitates, the bent legs scrabble,
and its eye, the one that can't turn away,
fish-egg black, stares and blinks.

Behind me, sitting in a chair, his head resting
in a pillow, a friend recites *Lycidas* to prove
it's not the tumor or the treatment that's wasted
what his memory captured years ago in school.

Never mind he drops more than a line
or two. It's not a *lean and flashy songs* he sings,
though that's what he'd prefer—his hair
wispy, his head misshapen.

Beyond the window, the wind shakes down
the dogwood petals, beetles drown in sap,
and bees paint themselves with pollen. "Get up! Fly away!"
my caption urges. "Get up, if you can!"

THE WATCH

Three days after our friend died,
having dropped to his knees
at the feet of his teammates,
we are sitting in a long,
narrow, windowless chapel,
staring at his casket
that runs parallel to the pews.
It's like a balance beam
or a bench you could sit on—
floral sprays around it,
a wooden lectern behind,
and a priest nobody knew,
a man I'd seen in the parking lot,
pulling on a beret and stamping out
a cigarette, all in one move,
as he emerged from his car,
holding a black book.
And now he is reassuring us
that our friend is in
a better place, that God,
too soon, has called him home,
a mystery faith endures.
Occasionally he looks down
to check his watch, the habit
of a man who always has
a next place to be, which must be why
he barely stays to finish the job.

Our friend

had the most beautiful voice
and his guitar was as cool
and smart, soulful
in its registers. When he played,
he gave his body to the music,
his eyes closed sometimes and his head bent,
sheltering what he made of himself,
his fingers knowing the next place
and the next—his voice, too—
taking each of us with him.

THE MISSING MOUNTAIN

Cars could reach the mountain's saddle,
a notch between two peaks, and there
survey the grid of lighted streets,
a bursting net of beads and sequins,
a straining movement cruising for release.

"As far as the eye could see," though
few cared to look, was across the valley
to the other mountain, whose ridge
stood gaffed with broadcast towers, bright
harpoons quivering out our songs.

"Oh, wouldn't it be nice," the Beach Boys
harmonized. And it was. Sometimes I saw
the Milky Way invade the grid, Andromeda,
Draco, and great Betelgeuse bridging
the avenues and lanes, filling up acres

of vast parking lots. Sometimes I stared
powerfully into space where glowworms
of matter spun in pinwheels of gas.
What did it mean to be alive?
a voice asked. What did it mean

to have a voice speaking from inside?
Once I found a cockpit canopy from
a fighter jet in my neighbor's yard,
where it had fallen from the sky.
No one ever claimed it, such a large,

specific, useless thing, like the shoe
a giant leaves behind, like a mountain
from childhood—missing or pulverized—
it leaves a shape that once you see it
overwhelms the mind or makes a cloud

that is the shape of what the mountain was,
the sea floor covered with the sea.
"Oh, wouldn't it be nice," I used to sing,
and the mountains all around me answered,
but not the question I had asked.

SINGING, 5 A.M.

Yesterday when it began,
I think I laughed myself awake—
so perfect, and clear, so pre-recorded,
so much the birds of the neighborhood
doing what they're supposed to do.

And you waking next but not laughing,
not at all, not even aware yet
of how loud the morning was becoming.
But when I turned wanting to face you
and brushed your hip, we came alive
to the air—or the air enlivened us.

Well, it was dark. Neither of us could see,
though we were laughing,
which is what astonishment did to us,
even before we felt grateful
or dissatisfied, even before we knew
we'd been waiting—awake or asleep—for the birds,
so early and for what?

MINE OWN JOHN CLARE

He was the first person I knew who spoke to God
and to whom God replied. And he was the first person I knew
who had written the great works of whomever you might name—
mine own T. S. Eliot—though he affected no accent
and wore a shrunken Grateful Dead T-shirt.

It was not only madness that possessed him,
he had convictions and discernments, fine and fierce—
he rode a tricycle, small as it was,
back and forth from Pangea to the End of the World
with a stop at the San Andreas Fault, where he lifted it,

wheels spinning, over the crack that runs to the center of the earth,
meaning he had circled all night in an empty parking lot
until his brother tracked him down and took him home.
He had moods and passions: months corresponding
with Germaine Greer and the articles he wrote for *Rolling Stone*

that appeared confoundedly under bylines not his own.
Once he spoke of walking three days from the northern high country
to the southern valleys, and toward the end, lost, hungry, he heard
a voice telling him to eat the grass. *Grass contains*
the secret whisperings of love, he said. But you had to crop

the tips of the blades and you had to be on your knees
with your head bowed and your eyes closed, and your lips made
the bitter taste sweet. Sometimes when he talked like this
he was also crying, because, he explained, *the grass contained wild onion*
and other truthful pungencies God requires me to eat.

And sometimes—*look at me!*—he'd put his face so close to mine
I no longer saw him but the parts that he contained: pores
and blemishes, the cheek's sharp contours, and his eyes,
dark, filmy patches, watery with years of homelessness ahead
but alive, fierce, and, as I pulled away, unforgiving.

ELEGY FOR A LONG-DEAD FRIEND

Last night when you appeared
you brought the sacks of shoes
and folded clothes that stood
waiting in your garage
for someone else to remove
the day you died.

Because you were laid out
at the coroner's when I arrived
you couldn't know what I saw:
boots and sneakers, sandals
jammed in grocery bags, shirts
and pants no longer stylish.

Months before, what was it
you said? "Don't come around
here again." So why these visits?
Why the burden of this evidence?
And silent as you are
does your presence mean forgiveness?

There was also, you should know,
a flat tire that gave your car
a slouched, defeated look.
I saw it before I saw the discards.
In Dante's hell the souls
spend their time repaying themselves

with their own sins. He witnessed
their anguish but was rarely moved
and Virgil, never. Next time
you visit bring that tire,
wear it like a necklace,
and we'll set it on fire.

A LINE FROM ROBERT DESNOS USED TO COMMEMORATE GEORGE "SONNY" TOOK-THE-SHIELD, FORT BELKNAP, MONTANA

I have dreamed of you so much,
you are the headless hawk
I found in a field, upturned
like a plow blade of feathers.
"Pick me up," you said, "so I might roost
as if I were the hawk."

I have dreamed of you so much,
a tree grew where I stood,
and grass rose up in flames
as if the hawk had sown a fire
from which its head appeared.
"Pick me up," it said.

I have dreamed of you so much
that now there is no dream,
no field or tree or fire,
only you roosting in the air.
"Pick me up," I say, "so I might roost
as if the world consumed my head."

BARDO

Dangerously frail is what his hand was like
when he showed up at our house,
three or four days after his death,
and stood at the foot of our bed.

Though we had expected him to appear
in some form, it was odd, the clarity
and precise decrepitude of his condition,
and how his hand, frail as it was,

lifted me from behind my head, up from the pillow,
so that no longer could I claim it was a dream,
nor deny that what your father wanted,
even with you sleeping next to me,

was to kiss me on the lips.
There was no refusing his anointing me
with what I was meant to bear of him
from where he was, present in the world,

a document loose from the archives
of form—not spectral, not corporeal—
in transit, though not between lives or bodies:
those lips on mine, then mine on yours.

from The Ledge (2000)

ARGOS

If you think Odysseus too strong and brave to cry,
that the god-loved, god-protected hero
when he returned to Ithaka disguised,
intent to check up on his wife

and candidly apprize the condition of his kingdom,
steeled himself resolutely against surprise
and came into his land cold-hearted, clear-eyed,
ready for revenge—then you read Homer as I first did,

too fast, knowing you'd be tested for plot
and major happenings, skimming forward to the massacre,
the shambles engineered with Telémakhos
by turning beggar and taking up the challenge of the bow.

Reading this way you probably missed the tear
Odysseus shed for his decrepit dog, Argos,
who's nothing but a bag of bones asleep atop
a refuse pile outside the palace gates. The dog is not

a god in earthly clothes but in its own disguise
of death and destitution is more like Ithaka itself.
And if you returned home after twenty years
you might weep for the hunting dog

you long ago abandoned, rising from the garbage
of its bed, its instinct of recognition still intact,
enough will to wag its tail, lift its head, but little more.
Years ago, you had the chance to read that page more closely

but instead you raced ahead, like Odysseus, cocksure
with your plan. Now the past is what you study,
where guile and speed give over to grief so you might stop,
and desiring to weep, weep more deeply.

MY CRUCIFIXION

Not blasphemy so much as curiosity
and imitation suggested I lie faceup
and naked on my bedroom floor,
arms stretched out like His,

feet crossed at the ankles,
and my head lolling in that familiar
defeated way, while my sisters worked
with toy wooden hammers to drive

imagined spikes through my hands and feet.
A spiritual exercise? I don't think so.
For unlike Christ my boy-size penis stiffened
like one of Satan's fingers.

I was dying a savior's death and yet
what my sisters called my "thing"
struggled against extinction
as if its resurrection could not be held off

by this playful holy torture, nor stopped
except by the arrival of my parents,
who stood above us suddenly like prelates,
home early from their supper club,

stunned, but not astonished, to find
the babysitter asleep and the inquisitive
nature of our heathenish hearts amok
in murderous pageantry.

THE WORD

"Gentlemen," the detention proctor
would begin, "you may recall Sisyphus
had a difficult life. He had to roll
a stone bigger than his own person
up a hill, et cetera, et cetera." And some
of us remembered Sisyphus from our defaced
Edith Hamiltons and some of us didn't.

Each of us deserved worse than we'd been given
for so much less than what we'd done
had been discovered. The proctor, a Jesuit,
never fit his punishments to our crimes.
"The idea of it," he said, "lacked elegance,"
though what kind of elegance he found
in a half-filled class of laggards

and reprobates I never understood, and so
we took our refresher on Sisyphus and waited
for him to assign "the word." The word—our stone—
we had to roll, neatly, as if out of a ballpoint pen,
five, six, seven hundred times.
A root ball of a word not impossible to spell
but a tangled mess to write: "Egypt," "gypsy," or "pygmy."

Unlike Sisyphus we had only an hour to complete
the task, though the proctor claimed he had
all the time in the world, until hell froze over.

Except he didn't say "hell." He said, "H-E-
double-toothpicks," as if to prove his boast
he'd never cursed, even once in his life, or as if to show

a word was the thing itself, not a stand-in
or a proctor to experience, not the near occasion
but *the* occasion. He was Christ's structuralist who doubled
as the tennis coach, whose pock-scarred face trembled
when he prayed, who saw tears of blood in Mary's marble eyes.
"H-E-double-toothpicks in a handbasket, gentlemen,"
if we didn't stifle the smirks, put our noses

to the grindstone, shoulders to the wheel, and wipe
the tarnish off the silver platter on which
we'd been handed our lives. Some of us perfected
a technique with two pens and some worked like monks
to illuminate the text with obscene hidden words.
We were subversive even as we suffered
our mild subversion, turning the torturer's delight

into the tortured's uncomfortable pleasure. We didn't know
"Jesuit" was a synonym for "sophist." We didn't know
what "sophist" meant, though now it's clear
how simple our deceptions were, our lies
like momentary lapses, and clearer still how the proctor's
skill at finding the cramp-producing words
was just a facet of a nature controlled

by a larger system of denial and forgiveness
that kept what seemed to torture him
so real it was a sin to say or spell.

THE FARRIER

The book is in my hands then his.
The desk, the lamp, the carpet fragment,
the pictures of the poets on the wall,
and then the window, and out beyond
the window, the land drops off steeply
to the river. The river winds into the sound
and the sound into the ocean. The book
we are reading is not the thing we pass
between us. The book we are reading
has not been written. It won't contain
"The Poem of Two Friends." It won't be called
"Teacher & Student," even now that one of us
is old, the other idling fluidly in middle age:
the book won't be written.

So how will we sort
the hammer and tongs? Who will wear
the bright bandanna around his head
or forge the useless shoe?
What is the sound the anvil
no longer makes?

The worked iron
cools in its own steam. It's night
beyond the window. Inside, the light
is bright enough for reading.
A mist spreads upward from the river.
The book is in his hand then mine.

GHAZAL

When I was young I couldn't wait to leave home
and then I went away to make the world my home.

In England a poet's wife suggested a word for what I felt,
"*heimweh.*" German for homesickness even when you're home.

The agoraphobe and claustrophobe respectively
cannot bear to leave or stay inside their home.

Our day-old-son wrapped in a blanket in your arms
and I'm in the car waiting to take both of you home.

Mortgage means "dead pledge." To buy a house
you need one. A house can be mistaken for a home.

It won't be hard to name the poet who wrote a sonnet sequence
about his mother and father. He called it "The Broken Home."

A shovel, rake, and pickax hang inside my neighbor's garage.
Like a god he has ordered the chaos of his home.

Never let me forget: colliers mine coal. Michael's an angel.
In heaven as on earth the coal of grief warms the soul's home.

ALL SOULS

A few of us—Hillary Clinton, Vlad Dracula,
Oprah Winfrey, and Trotsky—peer through
the kitchen window at a raccoon perched
outside on a picnic table where it picks

over chips, veggies, olives and a chunk of pâté.
Behind us others crowd the hallway, many more
dance in the living room. Trotsky fusses with the bloody
screwdriver puttied to her forehead.

Hillary Clinton, whose voice is the rumble
of a bowling ball, whose hands are hairy
to the third knuckle, lifts his rubber chin to announce,
"What a perfect mask it has!" While the Count

whistling through his plastic fangs says, "Oh,
and a nose like a chef." Then one by one
the other masks join in: "Tail of a gambler,"
"a swashbuckler's hips," "feet of a cat burglar."

Trotsky scratches herself beneath her skirt
and Hillary, whose lederhosen are so tight they form a codpiece,
wraps his legs around Trotsky's leg and humps like a dog.
Dracula and Oprah, the married hosts, hold hands

and then let go. Meanwhile the raccoon squats on
the gherkins, extracts pimentos from olives, and sniffs
abandoned cups of beer. A ghoul in the living room
turns the music up and the house becomes a drum.

The windows buzz, "Who do you love? Who do you love?"
the singer sings. Our feathered arms, our stockinged legs.
The intricate paws, the filleting tongue.
We love what we are; we love what we've become.

BRAVE SPARROW

whose home is in the straw
and baling twine threaded
in the slots of a roof vent

who guards a tiny ledge
against the starlings
that cruise the neighborhood

whose heart is smaller
than a heart should be,
whose feathers stiffen

like an arrow fret to quicken
the hydraulics of its wings,
stay there on the metal

ledge, widen your alarming
beak, but do not flee as others have
to the black walnut vaulting

overhead. Do not move outside
the world you've made
from baling twine and straw.

The isolated starling fears
the crows, the crows gang up
to rout a hawk. The hawk

is cold. And cold is what
a larger heart maintains.
The owl at dusk and dawn,

far off, unseen, but audible,
repeats its syncopated intervals,
a song that's not a cry

but a whisper rising from concentric
rings of water spreading out across
the surface of a catchment pond.

It asks, "Who are you? Who
are you?" but no one knows.
Stay where you are, nervous, jittery.

Move your small head a hundred
ways, a hundred times, keep
paying attention to the terrifying

world. And if you see the robins
in their dirty orange vests
patrolling the yard like thugs,

forget about the worm. Starve
yourself, or from the air inhale
the water you may need, digest

the dust. And what the promiscuous
cat and jaybirds do, let them
do it, let them dart and snipe,

let them sound like others.
They sleep when the owl sends
out its encircling question.

Stay where you are, you lit fuse,
you dull spark of saltpeter and sulfur.

PAY-PER-VIEW

Maybe you saw this as I did in a smoke-free
suite of the Allard Hotel in Chicago,
late in the afternoon, an hour away from drinks,
then dinner with a friend, after a long day of meetings.

Like me you clicked on the TV, surfed through
weather, CNN, and local news before stopping
at a woman with hair the color
of embalming fluid—a rose hips red.

She held up a pheasant by its legs in one hand
and a chicken in the same fashion with the other.
Both of the birds had been decapitated, plucked,
maybe even oiled, for they shone and glistened.

The pheasant was longer, leaner than the chicken
and, through the sheen, its skin was a whitish-gray
like asphalt dusted with snow. The chicken, robust,
jaundice-colored, hung swollen and fat. The woman placed

each fowl on its own large cutting board. A row of knives
lay waiting, but before she began dressing the birds
I changed channels, once, twice, and then rapidly,
turning the screen into a flip book, a cavalcade of images:

the U.S. Congress, a diamond necklace rotating in mid-air,
a bowling ball smashing silently into pins, and Lotto numbers,
as if they were verses from apocrypha, flashed above a blowup of
a check made out to *John Doe* for *Thirty Million Dollars and No One Hundredths.*

Occasionally the screen filled with bands of houndstooth or plaid,
scrambled colors behind which figures moved and a steady droning
music played, the kind the Harpies might have made for Sisyphus
each time he reached the hilltop. Beneath the music

and behind the meadowy zippers of color, I heard moaning,
a held-in keening, and staring hard, trying to locate
the sound in the bright reticulating light, I saw a man morph,
his head long, Martian green, arms without hands, legs

as malleable as mercury and then, as if engrafted to him or giving
birth to his form and deformation, a woman. Zeus made Pandora
from clay and had the four Winds fill her with life. She was not
a real woman but a god's vengeful fantasy of beauty.

And now those winged souls that once escaped
from her exquisite jar—the shadows of our pains, the venom
carriers of our desires—assemble an erotic chaos on the screen.
Delusive hope, which grows the liver back from the shreds

and tatters of the demons' feeding, entered me as perhaps
it enters you—a dryness in the throat, a conviction fed by
a yearning that in time the obscure and pleasure-giving bodies
would emerge clear and free.

CERBERUS

He was the yard dog's yard dog.
His heads accessorized with snakes.
His tail a scorpion's, and his slaver
a seed bank for hell's herbarium.
And his bites were worse than his barks.

What did he do in the underworld
except to guard the stairs leading
from the bitter tide-lap of the Styx?
How did he spend his days in the darkness
where only the dead can see?

His rheum-yellow eyes. His chainmail ears
larger than a basset's. Slower than Charon
at sorting the dead from the living—
yet more accurate, for like the dog
he was, he knew the various scents from the world above:

the grasses and tree bark, scat tracks,
the sweet acrid talc of dried piss. He knew
the dirt-under-the-nail smell of the desperate digging
from the buried-alive, the iron-on-the-tongue
of the licked wound. As ugly as he was,

he had exquisite breeding, a species unto himself.
The stud who would never have a mate. His cock,
a huge suppurating rudder, stirred the sulfuric
ocean of his realm; a homing device like his anger,
uncircumcised, guiding, probing, a love that could kill.

PAX GEOLOGICA

Last night the world's rifts, the ridges
that lie under the oceans, entered my dream,
seams and wounds of creation that spread
and subduct, whose monumental movement
makes mountains, erupts volcanoes,
and sets continents adrift.

In that peaceful destruction the possessions
of our house lay scattered on the floor
like a collection of basalt, glassine,
brittle from cooling, shaped like pillows
and sheets and columns from the temple
of the world's beginnings.

But out beyond the talus walls, over the caldera's edge,
the earth's manufacture of abyss slipped by
slowly. That was the night's upwelling, and in it
the sheer transparent creatures coalesced,
rafts of stellar luminescence—red, blue, and green—
deep, beyond reach, but in the world.

from The Neighbor (1995)

ARCHIMEDES

The name of the trailer
was "Lil'l Dude,"
the engine an Evinrude,
the boat a Glassport,

and under the yellow
bug-light of the carport
across the street,
my neighbor proved

his boast that with one
finger under the tongue
of the trailer,
he could lift the boat,

raise the bow as high
as his chest and haul
the rig by slow steps
onto the drive where

his pick-up idled,
and its running lights,
orange and yellow,
trimmed the camper shell.

The name of the camper
was "Six Pac," the truck
"Apache." Gerry cans
and butane tanks lashed

to the bumper and wheel
wells, and when he lowered
the trailer onto
the chrome sphere

of the hitch, the ball
and socket clicked.
He wrapped the safety
chains, like ligaments,

around the mount bolted
to the chassis, then
checked the safety
on the winch.

Inside the truck,
he eased the handbrake off
and the whole rig,
on its own, rolled

into the street.
And later, on the lake,
he held the Coleman
lantern over the dark

water, and fish rose
to it as to the sun,
a ball of gas burning
in a silk mantel, a lung

bright, reflected in the housing
glass like the source
of good to which everything
from its darkness turns—

depths of water, depths
of earth—words rising
to join their things. A flensing
knife strapped to his belt,

blade and handle shaped
like a fish and the fish
in the water,
shaped like the knife.

2212 WEST FLOWER STREET

When I think of the man who lived in the house
behind ours and how he killed his wife
and then went into his own back yard,
a few short feet from my bedroom window,
and put the blue-black barrel of his 30.06
inside his mouth and pulled the trigger,
I don't think about how much of the barrel
he had to swallow before his fingers reached the trigger,
nor the bullet that passed out the back of his neck,
nor the wild orbit of blood that followed
his crazy dance before he collapsed in a clatter
over the trash cans, which woke me.

Instead I think of how quickly his neighbors restored
his humanity, remembering his passion
for stars which brought him into his yard
on clear nights, with a telescope and tripod,
or the way he stood in the alley in his rubber boots
and emptied the red slurry from his rock tumblers
before he washed the glassy chunks of agate
and petrified wood. And we remembered, too,
the goose-neck lamp on the kitchen table
that burned after dinner and how he worked
in its bright circle to fashion flies and lures.
The hook held firmly in a jeweler's vise,

while he wound the nylon thread around the haft
and feathers. And bending closer to the light,
he concentrated on tying the knots, pulling them tight
against the coiled threads. And bending closer still,
turning his head slightly toward the window,
his eyes lost in the dark yard, he took the thread ends
in his teeth and chewed them free. Perhaps he saw us
standing on the sidewalk watching him, perhaps he didn't.
He was a man so much involved with what he did,
and what he did was so much of his loneliness,
our presence didn't matter. No one's did.
So careful and precise were all his passions,

he must have felt the hook with its tiny barbs
against his lip, sharp and trigger-shaped.
It must have been a common danger for him—
the wet clear membrane of his mouth threatened
by the flies and lures, the beautiful enticements
he made with his own hands and the small loose
thread ends which clung to the roof of his mouth
and which he tried to spit out like an annoyance
that would choke him.

THE HOUSE OF BEING

Little house it is,
little yard for exercise:
fence and alley gate,
trellis holding passion
flowers, nectar for hummingbirds
and bees, nails and crown
of thorns, ivy webbed
by trap-door spiders,
brick steps set out
at intervals, kettle
barbecue and wood pile,
deck for drinks and meals,
roses clipped, beds
pruned, driveway leading
to a closed garage;
little yard for exercise,
häftlinge clipped
and shaved; lager gate
with slogan: *Work Makes Free*;
band that welcomes back
the work details; tattooed
numbers read like names,
bunks with occupants
by twos and threes;
languages: French
and Dutch, Polish,
Yiddish—*der Dolmetscher*:
the rubber truncheon,
the interpreter.

—

Little house it is
behind the house
we rent; little yard
where the woman
in her house-dress walks;
hummingbirds and spiders,
alley gate and fence,
nails and thorns,
worn path beneath
her feet, circuit
that she turns
and turns: barbecue,
garage; little yard,
little house, the past
a language she can't
misspeak: growls
and yelps, gears
of syllables and vowels,
frenzy of imperatives,
a *wortschatz* of shouts,
commands, Yiddish,
Polish, German—
der Dolmetscher
that everyone can understand.

—

House of language,
little exercise
behind the house,
the woman in her dress,
her hair a whitish
gorse, she shouts
commands, frenzy
of imperatives:
Work Makes Free—
the lager gate,
trap-door spiders,
kettle barbecue,
closed garage.

THE BARBER

Even in death he roams the yard in his boxer shorts,
plowing the push-mower through bermuda grass,
bullying it against the fence and tree trunks,
chipping its twisted blades on the patio's edge.

The chalky flint and orange spark of struck concrete
floats in the air, tastes like metal, smells
like the slow burn of hair on his electric clippers.
And smelling it, I feel the hot shoe of the shaver

as he guided it in a high arc around my ears,
then set the sharp toothy edge against my sideburns
to trim them square, and how he used his huge stomach
to butt the chair and his flat hand palming my head

to keep me still, pressing my chin down as he cleaned
the ragged wisps of hair along my neck.
A fat inconsolable man whose skill and pleasure
was to clip and shear, to make raw and stubble

all that grew in this world, expose the scalp,
the place of roots and nerves and make vulnerable,
there in the double mirrors of his shop, the long
stem-muscles of our necks. And so we hung below

his license in its cheap black frame, above the violet
light of the scissors shed with its glass jars
of germicide and the long, tapered combs soaking
in its blue iridescence. Gruff when he wasn't silent,

he was a neighbor to fear, yet we trusted him
beyond his anger, beyond his privacy. He was like a father
we could hate, a foil for our unspent vengeance,
though vengeance was always his. He sent us back

into the world burning and itching, alive with the horror
of closing eyes in the pinkish darkness
of his shop and having felt the horse-hair brush, talc-filled,
cloying, too sweet for boyhood, whisked across the face.

THE RANCHER

When he rises from his Naugahyde recliner
to shake your hand, he cups his fingers
behind his ear to catch your name.
He grips your hand to see if you're man

enough to date his daughter, and though
you're barely man enough, you've got
the strength to pass his test.
You meet his eyes that know exactly

how to judge a lamb or yearling's face
and what he sees in yours he doesn't trust.
How could he? When his daughter's dressed
and wearing make-up, he calls her cheap,

a floozie. His wife's her pimp.
He's not *bad*, his daughter tells you.
We're all women in this house
and Mom's such a bitch.

When he's drunk, he comes into her room
with what she calls his badger's muzzle
and sniffs her neck and shoulders.
But what's worse, she tells you, is when

she comes home from her dates and if he's
still awake, he lifts her dress or puts
his hand inside her Levis. And so each time
you came to pick her up, he looked at you

as both the one who'd save his daughter
and use her. He told you once, *she lies—*
don't trust her, and then, as if to prove it,
he led you to the service porch,

where a freezer, as large as a grave casing,
paralleled his beat-up truck. He propped
the freezer open with a piece of 2x4,
high enough so that the light inside

illumined rows and stacks of plastic bags,
clear, the contents burred with ice.
Each one contained what looked to you
like scallops, though larger. He reached inside,

knocked a bag loose with his fist,
then picked it up and said, *She'll do to you*
what I did to sheep to get these,
then threw the bag back in, closed the lid,

slapped you on the ass and squeezed you,
hard. You felt the badger's muzzle then,
prickly and wiry, his cheek like a shaved pelt,
and then heard what he said, a whisper,

You tell me what it's like with her
and I'll be glad to listen.

MISSION BOULEVARD

The headshops with their billowing cloth
canopies, red lights and bead curtains.
The girls in bikinis, trying on thin brass
bracelets, bells tied with leather straps
around their ankles. And the boys in their
baggies and jams, red and blue St. Christopher
medals around their necks. Everyone shuffling
barefoot or in water-buffalo sandals, hair
long, shaggy with salt, reddish or blond.
And there was that room in the back with black
lights where you picked out the posters
of Pig Pen and Castro, and the lady with too many
bracelets rolled them tightly into plastic sleeves.

And now years later you think what hope is there
for a secret life? or for the awkwardness
of taking out from your madras shorts the vinyl
football-shaped coin purse in which you'd carefully
folded your savings for just this purchase?
What hope is there for falling in love again
with that woman who took the money and handed back
the change smelling of incense and leather,
while you stared through the glass sales case
filled with pipes, hookahs and roach clips,
and the colorful packs of cigarette papers
displayed in a fan like the tail of an exotic bird.

THE STEAM ENGINE

Mystery of the green drapes drawn across the entrance
to the dining room. Cigarettes in brash ashtrays.
Gin in the ruby-tinted knobby crystal bottle
with its regal stopper that fit as heavy as a ball bearing

in my hand. Always in their house I felt
like a passenger who had missed his train, abandoned
in the unfamiliar scale of their living room.
The plaster roses that worked their way in chains

across the ceiling's curving vault were like incisions
on a giant's leg. Plugged with paint the petals
seemed arrested half-way in their bloom.
Whole days I spent in the great nothing-to-do

of their lives. My aunt sat with me on the floor
and traced her sun-spotted hands over the viny
and twisted patterns of her Persian rugs,
while my uncle, untethered from the green tube

of his oxygen tank, wheeled out the wobbly trolley
cart that held the steam engine: blunt black boiler
and brass connecting rods, bright steel wheels
and copper coal hopper. And in the hissing of his

tank's regulator, I heard the echo of his every breath
filling up the house, the long escaping sigh
of oxygen held off, unbreathed, so he could concentrate
on banking the tiny loaf of fuel inside the boiler grate.

And when the fuel was put in place, my aunt would light a match
beneath the grate until the pill glowed red.
Then she'd shut the boiler door and set the flue
and all of us would wait for the hiss, the steam to knot,

tightening, then knocking, so that the pistons started
shunting, sliding in their cylinders, rods and elbows
rounding on their wheels—a perfect demonstration,
a source of energy and motion that lacked a belt
or drive wheel to connect it to the world.

PICTURES DRAWN BY ATOMIC BOMB SURVIVORS

Catalogs of the burned: people, telephone poles,
steam engines, wires, pigs, horses—many horses.
And the smashed: windows, buildings, wagons, cars,
streetcars. And the screaming: children for mothers,
mothers for children, pleas for help, water, food.

All of this set down by amateurs thirty years later,
makes the "compelling subject" more symbolic
than real, a legend that never lives up to its facts:
how the day went dark, a black rain fell, and the air
sucked out from the air left a hollow silence before

the wind returned, a Typhoon of black, burned
and splintered things, flames from the nonflammable.
As well as strange apocalyptics: a cow's tail hanging on a wire.
A man, naked, standing in the dark rain, holding an eye
in one of his hands. All of it no stranger than a dream,

except it was no dream's strangeness to wake from,
no place in the world's future from which we might look
and see a hand, fingertips on fire, blue flames,
the fingers like candles burning to their joints,
a dark liquid running to the ground along the wrist.

Or how the larger destruction concealed the smallest regret:
a girl's scissors and lunchbox scattered
on her class-room floor, and the girl, after the blast,
picking herself up, sees them. And now beneath her
drawing writes: "Why didn't I stretch my hands out

to take them? Those scissors sent by a friend in Hawaii.
They were sharp, shiny, and would never rust."

LETTER FROM MRS. C. G. VOGT

I saw Crane, swimming strongly. . . . It is a scene I am unable to forget, even after all these years, and now I am glad to know why that tortured man made such a decision.

These great and gentle violent flaws,
like waves that build to peaks and break,
are not the explanation for our acts
but rather the source of those
compelling tortured things that reside in us
from birth. And so, if at the time

I saw him emerge on the *Orizaba's* deck—
topcoat over his pajamas—and watched him fold
his coat over the ship's rail and place
both hands along it and then raise himself
on his toes, and then drop back again,
before he vaulted over the railing

into the sea, if at that time I had known
the two "earliest surviving photographs
of Harold Hart Crane," I might have seen
in one his final frontward pose already
practiced—the child at twelve months
acquiring his balance from the arm of a chair.

And in the other, set already on the obscure mystery
of leaving, his back turned, head cocked down,
as he leans over a stool as if to watch
the buoys and lifeboats lowered to his grown
and desperate self, which he saw, swimming strongly,
and as if forever though never again.

THE WATER DREAM

Courage from my oldest son
who wore the tanks and mask
whose feet were purple webs,

whose eyes, blue behind the oval
lens, shone bold. His hair
a yellow sponge wrapped around

the regulator gauge. Outside
the world of dream he would have drowned,
and so I wondered at the graceful

flutter of his kick and how he bore
the apparatus, wore the leaded belt
and where he learned his skill,

or how he knew to circle there
where sand shelved off to rocks,
and where the rocks shimmered

in bottom light—an orange murk
of shape and bulk to which he pointed
with a gig, short-handled, meant

for frogs. And then he surfaced,
and turning on his back so he could lift
the mask, he said, *Mother is near*.

Then he dove and disappeared,
and in his absence something cold rose:
the feeling of an empty place

where fear intrudes, where death becomes
the dreamer's death or where an animal
long-tame transforms into a beast.

But where I swam, I heard the turbines
of the dam whine and hum along the bottom
of the lake—a sound, like pressure

in the ears, a sound of crushing weight,
a thing almost too literal to dream,
an exit song where light answered light,

and where I rose to the conscious shore,
feet down, dry above the edge of the reservoir,
and where I heard a voice inside me say,

Go out, go out and walk on the water
as if on the meniscus of this dream. Shadow
the shadow movement of your son.

But in the dream I never rose,
and all at once I found myself
beneath black water, made blacker

by the hull that bobbed above me.
The boat that held my family—
father, mother, sisters—stuck

at anchor, and the anchor lodged
in dark. What son would not
acquiesce to danger and carry

with him the anger that neutralized
his fear, pocket his blame,
like air, against his father

for having been sent down to do a job
his father should have done
and finding it impossible to do,

come up a gasping failure?
And what little company
I would have needed to give me

courage. What shadow presence
came last and late and with impatience:
a knife handed down to me, a sharp

blade and raw-hide handle to cut
the line and watch the boat turn
away from me, while the brass prop

unwound slowly in the drift,
and the hand above reached down
to take the knife.

from The Folded Heart (1989)

NORTH CORRIDOR

Living along the path
of these inconstant tracks
(a spur for shuttling coal),

we've learned to anticipate
the freight that pounds
at night and shakes our home

and stays in us as a dream
of something heavy stays,
foreboding and proximate

but always passing through.
So when a single boxcar
strayed one morning, chalk-

scrawled with siding codes,
creaking and sighing,
but also jingling like coins

in a collection box, we left
our house to stare at it.
And where it came to rest,

a prisoner of the crossing gates,
it stayed until the afternoon—
unclaimed, inscrutable,

locked with metal sealing tape.
Cars shunted around it,
over the rails. Children scaled

its laddered sides and hung
from its chain-locked wheel brake
and fit their necks inside

the couplings' claw-shaped
handcuffs. They did it
for a thrill, for fun,

though no one laughed. Then
in the afternoon two railway men
appeared in their blue truck

and carried long pole pry-jacks
to the wheels and slipped
the iron tongues along the rails

until with only their bodies
they fulcrummed the boxcar
to move just off the crossing,

where it stayed until that night.
When we heard the thrashing, the screech
of metal stretching from the dark

tree-thick right-of-way, it was as if
the mother of us all had come
to claim us, angry, staring us down

with her bright headlight, then butting
our heads, staggering the whole house
behind the engine's sudden lurch.

SPIDER TUMOR

When you first told me about
the black silk the body spins out,
like a terrible cocoon, I imagined
her brain was like a bright field
the size of a portable movie screen
and that a white cone of light
cut through the darkness of a room
to strike the blank surface hard
with the magnified whiskers and hookworms
of dust covering the projector's lens,

and even as you explained how one side
of your mother's head would be shaved
and little X's and O's inked on her cranium
by the radiologist, and, failing that,
holes might be drilled and isotopes
lowered into her brain to lodge near
the mass, even then I thought a spider
tumor was something we might blow off
the surface of a lens or rub away
with our shirttails. But this morning,

early to visit you at your mother's house,
I reached the door as she opened it, bending
for the newspaper. Startled, she clutched
her robe and held the folded paper
to cover her wigless, rune-etched skull.
The sun caught her full on the face
and for a moment I saw how beautiful
she had always been, girlish almost,
a countenance death seemed willing to reveal.
Perhaps it was the way the sun filled

the alcove of the porch that reminded me
of years ago when I knocked at the same door
and finding it open walked quietly
into the room where your father lay
on the blue couch. And as if we were suspended
in air, he motioned that I sit by him
and hear his little wish: a large man
who wanted one more time to wade
into the cold green water of a lake, tilt
back his head and float as light as weeds.

I sat and watched him skim his hand
across the carpet and twist the nap,
like seedpods, with his fingers,
before your mother found me and eased me
from the room, the way, this morning,
she eased me past her own death, through
the room with its blue couch, to the kitchen,
where you stood wet from a shower,
a towel wrapped around your waist
and the sunlight spinning a hazy web

in your hair. And standing there,
you were no one if not your father,
or his wish to wade out of the water,
out of its mercy and forgiveness,
and dispel the weave of death
which traps and magnifies us in the past
and hides from us the brave though startled
gestures that begin each day: the hand
that reaches down to pick the paper up,
the hand that reaches out to lead us past.

BURIAL

As if to prove death benefits the world
of protocols and attendants, the small
white headstones curve in beautiful arcs
over these green and gentle, tree-spaced
hills. Oak and beech and poplar drop
their leaves like service bars, bronze
and red and gold as thick as the gilded
leaf-scroll on the adjutant's visor.

The thick oak casket lies under a white
makeshift shed. The family sits in rows
of metal folding chairs. They are close
enough to touch the black valance that drops
in pleats beneath the coffin, but their hands
would have to pass between the legs of eight
men in long black coats. The men stand
tense and wound, like cocked winches, and hold

the flag that's stretched as tight as steel
yet floats above the casket like an illusionist's
wife. Up the hill musicians play taps.
The tuba turns to catch the sun and shines
like a brass air vent. Farther up
the hill white gloves slide up rifle stocks,
slam bolts shut and aim the barrels high.
Before the rifles' sharp reports,

the barrels bloom with smoke
and in the short delay, the dead man
is meant to pass from this world
to the next, though surely he's been gone
for days and returns now for the pure
circumstance, the final ceremony
that has the flag become his heart,
folded in its bulky triangle and handed

to his wife, who knows she's not to look
but, rather, lays it on her lap
and puts her hands on top and presses down
as if to keep the loud heart from beating loud.

THE PROBLEM

Awake in the dark, I counted the planes
that hung by thumbtacks and string from the ceiling.

I brought them out of their shadows with their names:
Hellcat, Spitfire, Messerschmitt and Zero.

They were part of a problem that made death fair.

Part promise, part gamble, the problem went like this:
How old must I be before I am old enough for my father to die?

The answer was always twenty-one—
a number impossible to imagine.

It made the world fair enough for sleep.

My father didn't die when I was twenty-one.
I didn't blame him. He didn't know that night after night

I had bargained away his life for sleep.

Now to calm my fear of my father's death,
I remember the delicate plastic landing gear

of those airplanes, their sharp axles protruding
from the hard, gray tires. You had to be careful

with the noxious glue. You had to put one drop
of it on a difficult place and then blow lightly

until the tire began to spin.

THE HEAVY LIGHT OF SHIFTING STARS

Some times the nite is the shape of a ear only it ain't a ear we know the shape of.
—Russell Hoban, *Riddley Walker*

The huge magnanimous stars are many things.
At night we lower window shades
to mute the sparkling circuitry of the universe;
at day the sun's clear mist, like beautiful
cabinetry, shrouds the workings of the sky.

Everything is hidden, everything is apparent,
so that light coming toward us, held
in the faces of our old regrets, is blue;
while the light passing away, blurred
by our stationary focus, is red.

We cannot see these colors with our eyes,
just as we cannot feel the sun pushing the stars
outward or bending the paths of their light.
Years ago, when the world was flat, and then even
when the world became round, light was light,

dark was dark, and now, now that the world
is almost nothing compared with all that is—
all that we know—light identifies each atom
of the universe, and darkness swallows stars
like a whirlpool at the heart of a galaxy.

The huge magnanimous stars are many things.
We look to the sky and ask, What has changed?
Everything. But nothing we can see, and our seeing
changes nothing, until we move, and moving
we become the light of our atoms moving.

FEEDBACK

You are down on your knees, but you are not praying.
You are holding the hollow body
of your cherrywood Gretsch Tennessean
guitar across your thighs,

and you are pressing the right side of your face
against the black grille of the Fender Bandmaster amp
whose ruby pilot light glows like a planet in the dark.
You are listening to the last chord that fades into the black

cone of the speaker, which is ridged and grooved
like the walls of Hell and leaves only a ghost vibration
in your ear. And you are waiting for your friend to lower
the tone arm of the black plastic GE Stereo

onto the grooves of the record so you can imitate
Blue Cheer, Quicksilver, Jefferson Airplane,
and curve your shoulders over the guitar like a bird
holding its wings in glide, while your friend

rocks and jerks, gives himself over to the pulse
that drives you deeper and deeper
to the center of your teenage hearts. You are raw
and born for the distortion that lives beyond your ears

in the darkness, and is too loud with fuzztone
and wah-wah pedal. And each note or chord you strike
in imitation is partially saved, suspended,
as you pull and pump the vibrato's thin blade

and stir the molecules of sound as your long hair
obscures your faces, and you recede deeper, more separate,
into your selves here in this world, on this earth,
in the converted garage with its brown Georgia-Pacific

paneling and green burlap curtains that hang
above the avocado-green carpet.

THE CAVE

I think of Plato and the limited technology
of his cave, the primitive projection
incapable of fast forward or reverse,
stop action or slo mo and the instant replay
that would have allowed him to verify,
once and for all, *Justice* or the *Good,*

such as the way my family did, hour upon hour
in the dark, watching films of my sister
diving, going over her failures and successes
like a school of philosophers, arguing
fiercely, pulling her up from the depths
of the blue water, feet first, her splash

blooming around her hips, then dying out
into a calm flat sheet as her fingertips appeared.
Sometimes we kept her suspended in her mimesis
of gainer and twist until the projector's lamp
burned blue with smoke and the smell of acetate
filled the room. Always from the shabby of armchairs

of our dialectic we corrected the imperfect
attitude of her toes, the tuck of her chin,
took her back to the awkward approach or weak
hurdle and everywhere restored the half-promise
of her form, so that each abstract gesture
performed in an instant of falling revealed

that fond liaison of time and movement,
the moment held in the air, the illusion
of something whole, something true.
And though what we saw on the screen would never
change, never submit to our arguments, we believed
we might see it more clearly and understand

that what we judge was a result of poor light
or the apparent size of things or the change
an element evokes, such as when we allowed her
to reenter the water and all at once her body
skewed with refraction, an effect we could not save
her from, though we hauled her up again and again.

from The Clasp (1986)

AQUARIUM

The trigger fish and painted queens
add curves to their everlasting circuits
to avoid the woman working in the aquarium.

Blue scuba tanks striped with yellow
lightning bolts, red fins, orange gloves,
black skin, transform her into a species,

jury-rigged, though a patch of tan skin
between calf and thigh, like the cutaway
in a diagram, shows human tendon and muscle

flexing as she pedals, wipes the aquarium
glass with a cloth or dusts mottled armatures
of fake coral with a long boot brush.

Behind her mask her eyes are clear and dry,
but ringed with black mascara. Larger,
lighter, than our grounded selves who wave

to her, she waves to us, spits her mouthpiece
out, smiles, and pulls a glove off with her
teeth, then fits it to the air hose. The glove

fills and rises like a blowfish. Disturbed
to be seen by what we see, unconsciously
we hold our breath and wait until the woman

returns the mouthpiece to her mouth before
we exhale, letting go the bubbles of our wonder
and fear of the world behind glass, which we press

against to follow the woman's upward swim
as she retrieves the glove that bobs orange
and optically fat, a cloud in the aquarium's sky.

WHITE STRAWBERRIES

In the photograph she is not always
standing at the edge of the mowed field
clutching a bouquet of weeds for the mulch,

her ripped Wellingtons glistening from damp
grass and striped socks showing beneath
rolled-up pants. No, sometimes she floats

in the hazy marsh gas that rises in the reeds
behind her and the sun fills her hair with flames
that catch in the distant mulberry.

I've seen her disappear when wasps hover for
the dark berries and the air is clear,
the light endless; or when she points to the fish-

monger crossing the garden, sole in each hand,
his palms bleeding from fine cuts and a pink
blush spreads at the edge of the wet fillets.

Perhaps all memory of that country enters
this photograph, like cows escaped from pasture,
because for her, I have no remorse; it was clear

between us. Like the white strawberries
she brought from the garden one day, small,
covered with a bristly down, and which I thought

unripe, but they were precious,
nothing but a pale sweetness in her hand.

IN KHABAROVSK

Mud rising through thin snow,
and a dull welder's light
shining from the fires on the ice below—
as if from this quiet and vista
memory started out as a bright sun
against the completely unremembered.
Just as in another part of the city,
the thin Ussuri bends to confluence,
and Lenin Prospect ends at a granite
esplanade, steep gardens
leveling to a beach. In summer
families watch fireworks rising
from ghost-lit barges: this
in a travel brochure in my pocket,
which also shows the snow-covered square
in front of Hotel Europe,
from which I gauged the bend of my first walk
to this bank, without memory,
where beyond the fires
lay the blue horizon of China
and the barges setting out from there,
the lumberers with their last loads
of stolen larch, magpies circling;
and all the exhalations of horses and men,
like warm beats against the cold,
moved immunely over the snapping ice.
Then it was only in the river's name, Amur,
and after a long time
came a memory of love.

BRUGES

I dreamt of a Flemish city
that quit all commerce, drained its canals
and filled the empty channels with tulips
and mushrooms, and I dreamt of Betadine,
the orange paint of a surgeon:

snow fell from the sky
and a woman dressed in a green rain slicker
disappeared in the grainy world across the canal.
Soon I was touching the lathered sides
of a shaggy draft horse
at the back of a blind alley.
Ice nettled the horse's belly
and a stench rose in the mist of melting snow.
I wanted to make my way past death,
to use the horse and its black harness
and stop the snow falling
or stop the woman in her last shimmering.

Near morning the dream returned: the horse, fetlock deep
in snow, too large to turn around in the alley,
a feed bag muzzling its mouth,
and its stench, the stench of death,
frightened me, for I was aware
that the woman in the green rain slicker
had entered the room, and without looking
I knew she was just a few days beyond her death,

coming to tell me that there is no way past,
fresh from surgery in a green gown,
her head painted orange,
while behind her in the hall,
snow kept falling.

TWO GIRLS IN A CHAIR

Of the childhood photographs my wife
has given me, my favorite has her sitting
in a black alumni chair;
a college's gold seal and part of a Latin motto
curve beneath her right ear.
She's eight or nine, hair bobbed, dressed
in a white T-shirt and black tights
that reach only mid-calf.

She holds a neighbor friend in her lap,
someone whose leotards are ripped at the knees.
My wife's arms wrap around her friend's waist,
and her friend's feet dangle over the lily-
and fern-patterned linoleum.

Often when I enter my room, I notice only
this photograph, wedged among others,
and have felt a surprise of recognition
in those childhood friends
who could not now remember each other's name,
cannot recall what day of a New England summer
ended or began their long affection.

THE CLASP

See, how in a meticulous calm
I close the jaws, fitting the teeth
of the clasp, and coil the pearls
on the dresser top like a serpent
lowered into sleep. If I unhinged
the mouth, the teeth would glimmer
in the mirror like pebbles caught
in a tide line, a necklace of chance
that would stretch miles over
bark and foam, skirting the washed-up
skeletons, the husks and rinds
that lie like a bowerbird's last
baubles of elegance and attraction.
Here is the spiny vertebrae I rattle
for humor, here the red bobber
of fidelity, and there the blue
sandal I hold out for love.
But I have only the tiny adder's head
clasp staring at me, whose coiled
body is a string of kelp, all
bladder and beads, and if I opened
the mouth of what I've lulled asleep,
the viper, on waking, might strike
what it first sees: me, its tail.
And to that mirror that returns
everything to salt and sand, I bring
the lethal sleep, remembering the serpent
came from pearls, safe in their shells in the sea.

New Poems (2021)

A MAN OF RUEFUL COUNTENANCE

I woke up in the desert, which does not mean I had come to my senses
but found, although I knew how to pray, I had nothing
  to pray with.

I had lived a chivalrous life, opening doors for women and children
and men, nodding my head for them to pass, offering my seat
  whenever I could.

Although the needle of my vision was true to the path of my calling,
staying on track required constant correction and a steady belief
  in my fellow humans.

A man like myself lives by quests, not crusades, and so I tore off
the tail of my shirt and tied it in knots
  to serve as a rosary.

If I had been a sinner, a criminal, or the thief of my own soul, I would have made
a scourge of my shoes, studded with spines, and flayed myself all the way
  to the skull of Golgotha.

But my sins have been mild and for that harder to cleanse, except by device
and resourcefulness, like the rosary I worry with my hands, its beads
  caressed by words from my lips.

The sun is hot on my skin. Penance is a circle and circular, like faith
overlaid on acts. When I get to the end, to the crucifix of matchsticks,
  I begin again with the Glory Be, the sorrowful or joyful mysteries.

It should be easier to love, more difficult to hate.
But looking up, I see the desert is full of people walking in circles,
saying the prayers they know how to say.

A TRUE STORY ABOUT A CAT AND A POSSUM

You can give a cat a name, but you can't call one your own.
Even if you feed him, even if in the below-zero of winter
he sleeps, as our stray, "Goofy," does, on a heated pad
inside a large Amazon.com box, covered with worn-out,
braided kitchen rugs and retired bath towels, and even
if he pretends to answer when you call, he's not your cat.

He's an emissary from the world of the lost, an émigré,
who wears the story of his dispossession in a torn,
cauliflower ear that is less an ear than a sonic periscope
detecting the softest signals of mice and vole. Its rakish bent
like a French beret—"Parlez-vous français, Monsieur Le Chat?"

"Only in your dreams," he meows back, stretching out two stiff legs
before he rolls over like a fat, orange, gargantuan tick.

And speaking of ticks, possums are great eaters of the deer tick
by way of grooming themselves, also consumers of snails, mice,
and rats, and impervious to rabies as well as various poisons
and venoms, including rattlesnake. Good partners in the ecology
of the garden, and like great poets and savants, prone to seizures
that leave them paralyzed, open-mouthed, an hour or more,
in a state over which they have no control.

That's how we found it,

under the full force of our car's headlights, "curled up," you could say,
on a storage bin, next to Goofy's Amazon house, looking homeless
in its nakedness—the thick, pink cordage of tail, hairless, electrocuted.
Other times, under the car's bright interrogation, we found it eating Goofy's food,
not even looking up or shying away, although once, like a spy, it hid
behind a plastic bucket, its anteater nostrils and one obsidian pearl eye visible.

BEE TO KEEPER

Crouching in your white screened hood
off to the side of the landing board, your hands
and arms gloved to the elbows like a falconer,
you don't look at me the way I look at you,

cautiously, gauging my mood, wondering
if now's the time to meddle or through
the blurring crosshatch of your veil
become mesmerized by my waggling signals.

No one knows us better than ourselves,
better than you know by your interventions,
whether it be the removal of a failing queen
or the extermination of her rivals—nothing

we would not have managed in our own time,
which doesn't mean we don't want the powdery
insecticide to treat the plague that's killing us
or the division of the colony that forestalls migration.

Your intelligence allows you to see further than we
who don't really see at all as much as gather
information trapped in light, and yet what makes us
nervous—clouds and wind and rain—dark weather

with its portentous drop in pressure—makes you
reluctant to provoke, knowing in your work
how easy it is to crush us, we, who are so many
we seem to care little about ourselves, making

your inadvertencies our deaths, literally, at your hands,
acts of self-forgiveness—such is a definition
of the greater good. And yet the scent released
when we're crushed incites us to attack.

Our fear, so much less than yours, means we'll find a way
to penetrate your gear, and when we do, we'll see who's
calmest—the feel of us on your skin, the sight of us
in your hood, our everywhere whirr of wings.

PORTRAIT OF TWO YOUNG COUPLES

The tallest wears an orange, paneled ski jacket
that will go in and out of style, another
a gray hooded sweatshirt, the third, a sweater
knit by a mother who had never knit before,

while the fourth stands apart with her camera.
Ivy climbing up the trunk of an oak tree adds green
to the drab, wet day. One of the three in the photo
will die young, but you can't tell who he or she will be.

Each smile at eternity with equal conviction,
as if nonchalance was a moment's arrogance.
The brick sidewalk where they stand, ruptured by roots,
is destined to become smooth cement, and decades later

when the snapshot falls loose from its album,
the couple still married wonders about the one
who took the picture, her whereabouts—such specific
interchangeable lives? All four had either just left

the basement apartment where the couple in the photo lived,
or they were returning; the day was beginning or ending,
distinctions no longer important, except for the dead one,
whose whereabouts, there between his friends, facing

his wife, who's not yet divorcée or widow, would never be in doubt,
never be less than it was that day, in the middle of going or
coming, all four caught in their unknown futures.

COLLOQUY WITH A POLISH AUNT

Very often the title occurs to me before anything else occurs to me. This is not uncommon.
—Wallace Stevens

When Stevens writes: "imagination is the will of things,"
it's an arrangement of words that creates an idea,
but the life of the idea comes from the mouth,
improbable as that mouth must be, of a Polish Aunt.

Whose aunt? What's Poland? The imagination
is the will of things. What comes from the mouth
of the Aunt is the life of an idea, an arrangement of words
as improbable as it must be.

The imagination creates an idea that comes from the mouth
of an improbable life, the will of things that must be—
a Polish Aunt, an arrangement of words:
her baggy pants, a chaperone of spring.

Improbable as the mouth must be of a Polish Aunt—
that chaperone of spring with baggy pants—
is the will of things that creates an idea
whose life comes from an arrangement of words.

Thus, clothed in blue, wearing fancy slippers and
holding a book, the Aunt speaks the will of words,
their improbable life, the imagination of things,
a colloquy of is.

THE SALVATION OF AMERICA

Flagstaff, Arizona, 1972

Gene, our foreman, drove a red Ford Ranchero and wore laundered Western shirts with pearl-snap pockets and cuffs, a belt buckle the size of Montana, where he was from, and round-toed cowboy boots. He smelled of bay rum and Brylcreem and waited in his cab for the dust to settle before he'd open the door. "Fuck" was his main form of encouragement and "I don't give a shit" his answer to everything *we* said about why the job was off schedule, and then he'd disappear for a while in the trailer where his Mormon bosses, who wore white hard hats, chastened him with their calm, terrifying, alien demeanors. Gene was an employee of Ken Cail Plumbing, who fired *him*, then the Mormons fired Ken, and all the rest of us were let go, including the welders from Lubbock. The rest of us: Ray Borst, John Likovich, a squirrely, acne-faced guy whose name I don't remember but who had dreams of becoming a classical guitarist, and Michael Collier.

Whenever I hear someone say we need businesses and corporations to solve America's problems, I see us standing in the deep, wide ditch blasted out of solid rock meant to carry water, gas, and sewer lines, looking up at Gene, Ken, and the Mormons, with their sick, despairing, hopeless, not-really-knowing-what-the-fuck-to-do expressions, except to have the four of us, teenagers, pre-apprentice plumbers, with long, stringy hair, each with a shovel, keep spreading popcorn-size volcanic cinders, wheelbarrowed from dump-truck loads, to cushion the pipe, hoping, but not having a clue, that when the ditch was filled the lines would bear the weight.

GOAT ON A PILE OF SCRAP LUMBER

He lowers his head like a fur-covered anvil,
as if he knows all things in the world change.
His eyes are bisected by a horizon line of yellow light.
You're wondering what might happen if you move closer.
There's a language we speak to ourselves and one we use for others.
I told you, he's lowered his head.
Nevertheless, you can see for yourself he's chewing.
What he swallows becomes his rumination.
I too was attracted to someone I did not understand.
With each other we were bestial—that's not too strong a word.
Although at first, at first, when our foreheads touched, we were curious.

CYCLIST BRAKING FOR TWO FOXES CROSSING A COUNTRY ROAD IN EARLY MORNING

One first dashing, right to left, looking over its shoulder,
then disappearing into a muddy farmyard.
The other following at an interval, dashing as well
but holding a creature in its mouth like a black sock.
The world begins, and the world ends.
The tube gorging the mouth of a friend in the ICU is an umbilicus.
Her good arm and hand restrained.
The fox drops what it carried at the edge of the road.
It doesn't look back at the body whose wings,
shouldered with bright red and yellow, unfold.
The bird's dead, but the foxes crossed safely.
Dead space in the airway. We can hardly breathe
for what our mouths hold.

MORNING CROWS IN A FRESH MOWN FIELD BEFORE RAIN

Three in a group, then one coming from a distance
to make four dividing into two scavenging pairs.

They waddle like ducks, dibble like robins.
This close to the earth they have nothing to say.

And yet as they bobble in a hands-behind-back
colloquy of feints and nods they are the ankle boots

of an idea gone missing, their laces threaded
through eyelets but left untied, accountants

of random expenditures, connoisseurs
of the worm's catacombs of waste; they limp eastward,

toward the mountains, covered in contractor bag
capes, one wiry boot then the other on the ground.

If they would stay just where they are all morning,
they'd be the monument to the history they're looking for.

HIS HIGHNESS'S DOG AT KEW

That's who I am—pampered, well fed,
trampling slack-leashed into the beds,
blooming or not, depositing my turds
and sprinkling tulip stalks
whose buds are like the bud I lick.

And though I look like a dust mop,
a four-legged moustache, trim my bangs,
and as fierce as an Assyrian sight hound,
I'll find my way back to Peritas or La Vega Real,
snout wet with the gore of human bowel.

But for now a squeaky, annoying yap
warns as well as a mastiff's bark.
Truth is, I'm weightless in a lap,
and, on a cold day, I like a cardigan,
at night, a stiff brush, all of which
sharpens the loneliness I feel.

So that's who I am,
and now if you don't mind, tell me,
whose dog are you?

PENN RELAYS

My father is searching his wrist,
patting with fingers that moments before
nervously fiddled the bedsheet's hem.
Those of us near see in his fidget
a body reading the braille of its dying.
But all my father wants is his wristwatch,
the one with PENN RELAYS running
around the face of the clock. It would give him
some comfort to wear, not that he knows
where he is, not that he cares about time,
but he's never not had it awake, strapped
to his wrist, not since he and his teammates
won what's engraved on the back:
Half-Mile Relay Championship of America 1937.

WINTER

What sun there is is a mood of headache,
an exposure to an afternoon's hard, window-putty glare,
without which night wouldn't be so welcomed,

wouldn't be the plush extinction of our plans,
as when a glove noticed on a sidewalk becomes advertised
on a fence paling—as if one good turn deserves a reunion.

If winter darkness is time taken away from light, then winter sun
is not quite what's meant by being low on the horizon,
nor coverlets of snow. Indeed, what in the branchless, leafless world remains?

"For whom," one might ask, as well as where, when, and how?
Light that merely grazes the shoulder, the way, in summer,
a bra strap hangs in a loop off a shoulder, hardly noticed?

Among those not waiting for the sun to guide them back
to the cleft maple to continue its excavation is the pileated woodpecker.
Where do any of them live this time of year?

And in the frozen, woody marrow of trunk, what are they grubbing?

OUR FELIX RANDAL

Coming back from the toilet where he'd been taken by two younger friends
who helped shimmy the diaper down his legs to ease him into place—
        "Now you can leave me," he said.

Coming back from the toilet where he'd been, and this is the word he used,
"unproductive," he gave them in the sheer difficulty of managing his body
        through the hall, two doors,

and then the twisting, skewing, almost out-of-control resettling in the bed,
an expectation of how soon he'd be dead and yet strong-sinewed
        to the end, alert, even though his eyes

answered elsewhere, as if he were standing on his toes to look over
a crowd to see where the line was going.
        They loved him and told him so.

"Let's not use that word, someone we know has already used it 12,453 times,"
by whom he meant a rival he loved who would outlive him,
        as they would, the self-assigned sons and acolytes

who one at a time said goodbye, and that's when he told them
something he believed true about each of them, now that love
        had been dispatched and he was undefended.

IN LIFE

I once believed we all have one chance to love deeply,
an opportunity not only in the business of flesh and heart
but in the loneliness of the soul, and if we miss it,
as I thought I had on June 15, 1976, waking up in my room
that fronted Half-Moon Lane, Herne Hill, London,
listening to the dieseling idle of a nutcracker-red double-decker at its stop,
its loose-change-in-a-pocket vibration opening my eyes
to the fully revealed presence of a woman, sitting next to me,
holding in her hands a cup and saucer that she chimed with a spoon . . .

. . . and if we miss it, as I thought I had the week before, when
in the middle of the night, in the deepest most submerged hour
of sleep, my eyes opened to the ceiling light somehow on,
hanging, like a signal lantern, swinging, no longer
a pale-white-yellow but rouge-red, the filament inside
a clear pair of insect legs, twitching, the friction exploding the door
open, behind which a young girl entered sitting in a swivel chair
that went round and around and round, her hair, fanning out,
her mouth open but silent . . .

. . . and if we miss it?

When I was five and lay under a thin cloud of ether, I could see the blurred forms
of gods and goddesses as they reached through the mist to heal me.
They spoke indecipherably. I heard the clink of their tools.
I saw this not by looking up from where I lay but down from above,
and not with my eyes but with a penetrating embrace.
The body can see what it feels. It must go out of itself.
And when it returns? No one should ever experience such loneliness.

BLUEBIRDS

If I had wings the deep blue tint of a mountain sky
after sunset I would be more vain
than I am already. I might believe
that my happiness is conditioned on being
observed and admired. Whereas birds
are rarely content, so we must be happy for them,
especially this particular pair, nesting
in the limbless shaft of a maple tree.
They have russet and white breasts
that make them look regal and calm as they perch.
Their blue, which predominates, is also a royal color.
How lucky they are to have found an opening
of the right size and distance from the ground
they need in which for now to make their home.

POEM FOR A SIXTIETH BIRTHDAY

When I see you coming up the drive,
    broad, striped headband covering
        your hair and ears, your legs solid,
tan from a million miles of walking,

and when I see your arms
    swinging at your sides,
        hands loose at mid-thigh, a T-shirt
appearing to be clothespinned to your shoulders,

and maybe hear your shoes scuff
    and drag or maybe hear you stop
        to look back from where you'd been
to check again the view of fields and river

you love more deeply than I,
    and when I hear you talking
        to the barn cat who trots to greet you
(like a cat acting like a dog),

or maybe you've stopped
    to pull weeds, re-stake a toppling
        hollyhock, then I know
that forgetting, as if you'd never

been away, had been crucial
    to seeing in your absence
        how much I missed you.

TODAY I CAN WRITE

Today I can write the happiest lines.

Write, for example, "The morning grows bright,
and the sun warms the sky and the earth.

The day makes a blue clock of its light."

Today I can write the happiest lines.
I love her, and she loves me too.

Mornings like this we hold each other in our arms.
We kiss, make love, kiss, and make love.

She loves me, and I love her too.
How could I have not touched her lips with my tongue?

Today I can write the happiest lines.
The wonder of having each other. To feel we are complete.

To hear the endless day, ever more endless with her.
And our words enter us, stirring us like wind rustling leaves.

What does it matter we might not see each other all day?
The morning grows bright as we kiss and make love.

This is everything. How we touch, here and now, not later.
Let's not ask for more happiness than this.

I had an idea of who I was looking for before I found her.
My heart blind, unfeeling, before I saw her.

The same morning made the same trees green.
Many years have passed, many things have changed.

But I love her, that's certain. How I love her.
My voice finds its voice when she listens to me.

Another? Yes, for all lovers there's always another.
A voice, a bright body, a face. Years pass.

Once looking for her, I lost her. Once she lost me.
Years pass. I love her. She loves me.

Mornings like this, we hold each other in our arms.
Today I can write the happiest lines.

I don't need words to tell me what I feel, nor my heart.
What I feel I feel when she holds me in her arms.

TO THE MUSE OF DYING

When I'm lying like my father lay,
mouth agape in the tilted bed,
surrounded by family,
if I have the luck to lie like that
and overhear them talk about
the different routes that brought them
home to be with him, his children
catching up on their children's cousins
or the recent trips they've taken,
all the while attentive to his needs
(lip balm for his lips or a nudge
to keep his hand from slipping off his chest),
if I should be like him, unable
to say a final word or smile
in recognition when the last
of us arrived to kiss his forehead,
don't let me think what I'm thinking now
—my powers of attention already waning,
my generosity running out—that everything
I've done I've done for nothing.
No, if I have the chance to lie
like my father lay, listening
to those around me, whoever
they might be, all I want
is for them to keep calling
my name, the way my father's
was, gently, inquiringly—
"Robert" and "Dad"—
even past the moment
I am dead.

TREE BEYOND YOUR WINDOW

One day you look up, and all that's left of leaves
is a twisted trunk, thick at the base, an obelisk

split at the top like an ungulate's hoof, a shaft
riddled with holes, hopeful places for birds

to make their fastidious nests. And if you look closer,
you'll see a tortoise, head as big as a howitzer shell

and two legs, trying calmly to swim out
from the leathery bark of which it's made.

It wants to know, like an accuser in a dream,
what have you done with your life, and raising its rough,

amphibious hands, holding them out, implores you
to pull its ancient body from the tree.

NOTES

"Grandmother with Mink Stole, Sky Harbor Airport, Phoenix, Arizona, 1959": for Ellen Bryant Voigt.
"At the End of a Ninetieth Summer": for Lucille and Robert Collier.
"Doctor Friendly": for Stanley Plumly.
"History": for James Longenbach.
"The Bees of Deir Kifa": for Zein and Bilal El-amine.
"Laelaps": for Judith Cloud.
"Summer Anniversary": for Emmy and Bill Maxwell.
"Bird Crashing into Window": for Agha Shahid Ali.
"The Watch": for Dennis Casey.
"Bardo": for Ben Branch.
"The Farrier": for William Meredith.
"Pax Geologica": for John Delaney.
"Spider Tumor": for John Murphy.
"Goat on a Pile of Scrap Lumber": for Judy and Joe Powell.

—

"My Bishop": http://www.nytimes.com/2003/06/17/us/phoenix-bishop-arrested-in-fatal-hit-and-run-accident.html.

"The Storm" quotes lines 11 through 17 of John Berryman's "Winter Landscape," from *John Berryman: Collected Poems, 1937-1971, edited and introduced by Charles Thornbury* (New York: Farrar, Straus & Giroux, 1989).

"Boom Boom" responds to Pablo Neruda's "Infancia y poesía," from *Obras Completas,* 3rd ed. (Buenos Aires: Losada, 1968), 1:34

"Len Bias, a Bouquet of Flowers, and Ms. Brooks": The end words are taken from lines 5 and 6 of Gwendolyn Brooks's "The Last Quatrain of the Ballad of Emmett Till": "She kisses her killed boy. / And she is sorry." Len Bias, a University of Maryland basketball player, died of a drug overdose shortly after being drafted by the Boston Celtics.

"Bird Crashing into Window" employs a phrase from line 123 of John Milton's "Lycidas."

"A Line from Robert Desnos Used to Commemorate George 'Sonny' Took-the-Shield, Fort Belknap, Montana": George Took-the-Shield was fifty-three when he died of cancer. He was an Assiniboine instrumental in the repatriation of his ancestor's remains held by the Smithsonian Institution. He was an artist, writer, and poet.

"Today I Can Write" is based on W. S. Merwin's translation of Pablo Neruda's "Poem XX: Tonight I Can Write."